Praying Your Way through Luke's Gospel and the Acts of the Apostles

Praying Your Way through Luke's Gospel and the Acts of the Apostles

Mark G. Boyer

WIPF & STOCK · Eugene, Oregon

PRAYING YOUR WAY THROUGH LUKE'S GOSPEL AND THE ACTS OF THE APOSTLES

Copyright © 2015 Mark G. Boyer. All rights reserved. Except for brief quotations in critical publications or reviews, no part of this book may be reproduced in any manner without prior written permission from the publisher. Write: Permissions, Wipf and Stock Publishers, 199 W. 8th Ave., Suite 3, Eugene, OR 97401.

Wipf & Stock
An Imprint of Wipf and Stock Publishers
199 W. 8th Ave., Suite 3
Eugene, OR 97401

www.wipfandstock.com

ISBN 13: 978-1-4982-2858-9

Manufactured in the U.S.A.   09/16/2015

The Scripture quotations contained herein are from the *New Revised Standard Version Bible: Catholic Edition* copyright © 1993 and 1989 by the Division of Christian Education of the National Council of the Churches of Christ in the U.S. A. Used by permission. All rights reserved.

Quotations from the Catechism of the Catholic Church are taken from *Catechism of the Catholic Church* copyright © 1994 by the United States Catholic Conference—*Libreria Editrice Vaticana*. All rights reserved. Used with permission.

Dedicated to
Richard & Chris Kahl,
very good friends

Contents

Introduction | xi

Part 1: Prayer in Luke's Gospel | 1

People at Prayer | 1
(1:10): December 19; June 24 (Vigil)

Zechariah at Prayer | 3
(1:11–13): December 19; June 24 (Vigil)

Anna at Prayer | 4
(2:36–38): December 30; February 2

Jesus at Prayer | 5
(3:21–22): The Baptism of the Lord, Cycle C

Desert Prayer | 7
(5:15–16): Friday after Epiphany or January 11

Discernment Prayer | 8
(6:12–13): Tuesday of the Twenty-Third Week in Ordinary Time, Years I & II; October 28

Prayer for Adversaries | 10
(6:20, 27–28): Sixth Sunday in Ordinary Time, Cycle C; Wednesday of the Twenty-Third Week in Ordinary Time, Years I & II; Thursday of the Twenty-Third Week in Ordinary Time, Years I & II; November 17; December 23

Fasting and Prayer | 12
(6:33–35): Seventh Sunday in Ordinary Time, Cycle C; Thursday of the Twenty-Third Week in Ordinary Time, Years I & II; November 17; December 23

Prayer Alone | 13
(9:18): Twelfth Sunday in Ordinary Time, Cycle C; Friday of the Twenty-Fifth Week in Ordinary Time, Years I & II

Transfiguring Prayer | 15
(9:28–29): Second Sunday of Lent, Cycle C; August 6, Cycle C

Jesus' Prayer | 17
(10:21–22) Tuesday of the First Week of Advent, Years I & II

Praying Prayer | 19
(11:1–2): Seventeenth Sunday in Ordinary Time, Cycle C; Wednesday of the Twenty-Seventh Week in Ordinary Time, Years I & II

Pray Always | 21
(18:1, 6–8): Twenty-Ninth Sunday in Ordinary Time, Cycle C; Saturday of the Thirty-Second Week in Ordinary Time, Years I & II

Prayer Stance | 22
(18:10–11, 13–14): Thirtieth Sunday in Ordinary Time, Cycle C; Saturday of the Third Week of Lent, Years I & II

House of Prayer | 25
(19:45–46): Friday of the Thirty-Third Week in Ordinary Time, Years I & II

Alert Prayer | 27
(21:36): Saturday of the Thirty-Fourth Week in Ordinary Time, Years I & II

Prayer for Simon | 29
(22:31–32): Palm Sunday of the Lord's Passion, Cycle C

Earnest Prayer | 30
(22:40–45): Palm Sunday of the Lord's Passion, Cycle C

Forgiveness Prayer | 32
(23:32–34): Palm Sunday of the Lord's Passion, Cycle C

Abandonment Prayer | 33
(23:46): Palm Sunday of the Lord's Passion, Cycle C

Part 2: Prayer in the Acts of the Apostles | 35

Constant Prayer | 35
(1:13–14): Seventh Sunday of Easter, Cycle A; October 7

Replacement Prayer | 37
(1:23–26): Seventh Sunday of Easter, Cycle B; May 14

The Prayers | 39
(2:41–42): Second Sunday of Easter, Cycle A

Hour of Prayer | 41
(3:1–2): Wednesday of the Octave of Easter, Years I & II; June 29 (Vigil)

Prayer for Boldness | 43
(4:24–25a, 26–31): Monday of the Second Week of Easter, Years I & II

Serving Prayer | 45
(6:2–4): Fifth Sunday of Easter, Cycle A; Saturday of the Second Week of Easter, Years I & II

Stephen's Prayer | 47
(6:8–10, 12; 7:51, 54, 58–60): Monday and Tuesday of the Third Week of Easter, Years I & II; December 26

Prayer for the Holy Spirit | 49
(8:14–16): Sixth Sunday of Easter, Cycle A

Prayer Gift | 50
(8:18–20, 22)

Saul at Prayer | 52
(9:10–12): Friday of the Third Week of Easter, Years I & II; January 25 (Second Option)

Peter's Prayer | 54
(9:36–37a, 40): Saturday of the Third Week of Easter, Years I & II

Prayerful Cornelius | 55
(10:1–4)

Peter's Visionary Prayer | 57
(10:9–11, 16–17a, 19–20)

Retelling Visionary Prayer | 60
(11:2–5a, 18)

Praying Church | 62
(12:1–5): Monday of the Fourth Week of Easter, Years I & II

Commissioning Prayer | 64
(13:1–4)

Strengthening Prayer | 67
(14:22–23): Fifth Sunday of Easter, Cycle C; Tuesday of the Fifth Week of Easter, Years I & II

Place of Prayer | 68
(16:13–14, 16): Monday of the Sixth Week of Easter, Years I & II

Sung Prayer | 70
(16:25–26, 29–31): Tuesday of the Sixth Week of Easter, Years I & II

Kneeling Prayer | 72
(20:36–38a): Wednesday of the Seventh Week of Easter, Years I & II

Beach Prayer | 74
(21:4–6)

Prayer Trance | 75
(22:17–19)

Prayer for More Believers | 77
(26:27–29, 31–32)

Prayer for Day | 79
(27:29)

Healing Prayer | 81
(28:7–9)

Other Books by Mark G. Boyer | 83
Index of Biblical Quotations | 85

Introduction

PRAYER

Prayer is the heart of the Christian life. In fact, the *Catechism of the Catholic Church* says, ". . . [I]t is the heart that prays."[1] Thus, prayer is the raising of the heart to God. "Christian prayer is a covenant relationship between God and man [and woman] in Christ," states the Catechism.[2] "It is the action of God and of man [and woman], springing forth from both the Holy Spirit and ourselves, wholly directed to the Father, in union with the human will of the Son of God made man."[3]

Traditionally, prayer is divided into five forms. First, blessing prayer, which "expresses the basic movement of Christian prayer, . . . is an encounter between God and man [and woman];"[4] blessing prayer creates in people an attitude of adoration. The second form of prayer is petition, which "expresses awareness of [one's] relationship with God,"[5] namely, as a creature seeking the forgiveness of the Creator, searching for his kingdom, and trusting that he knows one's every need.

1. *Catechism*, par. 2562.
2. Ibid., par. 2564.
3. Ibid.
4. Ibid., par. 2626.
5. Ibid., par. 2629.

Introduction

The third form of prayer is intercession, a form of the prayer of petition. Intercessory prayer is "asking on behalf of another;"[6] it is "characteristic of a heart attuned to God's mercy."[7] Prayer of thanksgiving is the fourth form of prayer in which the pray-er presents every event of his or her life as "an offering of thanksgiving" to God.[8] The fifth or last form of prayer is praise, "which recognizes most immediately that God is God."[9] The *Catechism* says, "It lauds God for his own sake and gives him glory, quite beyond what he does, but simply because HE IS."[10]

PRAYER IN LUKE'S GOSPEL AND THE ACTS OF THE APOSTLES

For the author of Luke's Gospel and the Acts of the Apostles, prayer is the habit of being in the presence of God. The author of Luke's Gospel posits several unique characteristics of Jesus which are applied to the apostles in the Acts, the second volume of a two-volume work. The primary characteristic is that Jesus eats a lot of meals. While he eats meals in the other gospels, he eats more meals in Luke's Gospel. In the Acts of the Apostles, the apostles share the same characteristic with Jesus.

The second primary way in which Jesus is characterized in Luke's Gospel is that of a pray-er. Before every major event in his life, the Lukan Jesus is found praying, being in the presence of God. Likewise in the Acts of the Apostles, before any major decision the apostles are portrayed praying, being in God's presence.

Prayer is the topic of this book. It is titled *Praying Your Way through Luke's Gospel and the Acts of the Apostles* because it highlights the passages where Jesus is found praying in the gospel and where the apostles are found praying in the Acts.

---

6. Ibid., par. 2635.
7. Ibid.
8. Ibid., par. 2638.
9. Ibid., par. 2639.
10. Ibid.

Introduction

Luke's Gospel and the Acts of the Apostles, the largest work in the Christian Bible (New Testament), were written near the end of the first century for an upper class Gentile audience. As what is now known as Christianity made its way through the Roman Empire, it also made its way into the homes and lives of the elite. The writer of both books may have had a patron named Theophilus, who financially supported the production of the books. Theophilus' name appears at the beginning of the Gospel (1:3) and at the beginning of the Acts (1:1). Or, as his name implies (God-lover), he may be any Gentile (or all Gentiles as a corporate whole) who is interested in an orderly account of the events concerning Jesus of Nazareth and the group of apostles who followed him.

For many people prayer is talking to God. And in some ways that is true. But prayer is also listening to God, being in God's presence, according to the Luke-Acts author. Moreso, prayer is calling upon and listening to the Holy Spirit, who guides Jesus from the first moment of his conception in Luke's Gospel and guides the apostles from Pentecost in the Acts. In other words, prayer is a dialogue between people and God through the Holy Spirit; it involves both talking and listening; it involves both people and God being present to each other.

While we do not have the words of most of Jesus' prayers, we have the example he gives in Luke's Gospel, and we have the example the apostles give in the Acts of the Apostles. From the examples, the reader concludes that prayer should be a part of the life of any Christian—that is, any person who claims to be a follower of Christ. If Jesus himself prayed—spoke and listened to God—then how can his followers do any less?

STRUCTURE OF THE BOOK

This book is designed to be used by individuals for private study and prayer and by homilists for study, prayer, and preaching. For both the aid of individuals and homilists, the table of contents lists when specific biblical passages are used in the Lectionary.

Introduction

The Lectionary, a book of Scripture texts for every day of the year, contains three cycles of readings for Sundays, designated A (2017, 2020, 2023, etc.), B (2015, 2018, 2021, etc.), and C (2016, 2019, 2022) and two cycles for weekdays, designated Year I (odd numbered years) and Year II (even numbered years). There are also special solemnities, feasts, memorials, and optional memorials that interrupt the Sunday and weekday cycles. These are indicated by a date in the table of contents.

This book is divided into two parts. The first part examines prayer in Luke's Gospel. Part two examines prayer in the Acts of the Apostles. A five-part exercise is offered for every one of the forty-five entries.

1. A title is given to the exercise, disclosing the focus of the entry.

2. A few verses of Scripture are provided. I recommend that the reader find the passage in his or her Bible and read it in its broader context. The passage features Jesus praying from Luke's Gospel or the apostles praying from the Acts of the Apostles.

3. A reflective study follows the Scripture selection. The reflection presents some of the context for the biblical passage. It also applies modern forms of biblical criticism in order to surface its meaning. Where appropriate, it provides material from part four—"Christian Prayer"—of the *Catechism of the Catholic Church*. As it offers the individual and the homilist valuable background and contextual information, the reflection yields new perspectives for personal study on and suggestions for application of the biblical passage.

   Throughout the reflections, I use the masculine pronoun for God, LORD, LORD God, etc. I am well aware that God is neither male nor female, but in order to avoid the repetition of nouns over and over again, I employ male pronouns, as they are also used throughout most biblical translations.

4. The reflection is followed by a question for personal meditation. The question functions as a guide for personal

Introduction

appropriation of the message of the Scripture passage, thus leading the reader into prayer. The reader can use the question as a journaling exercise. The homilist can use the question as a basis for a sermon or brief homily.

5. A prayer concludes the exercise and summarizes the original theme announced in the title, which was studied and explored in the reflection and which served as the foundation for the meditation.

USING THIS BOOK

This book can be used at any time during the liturgical year that a person desires to develop further his or her life of prayer. For example, its forty-five entries can serve to deepen one's life of prayer through the Advent-Christmas Season, which consists of about forty to forty-five days. It can be used during Lent's forty-four days of preparation for the Paschal Triduum and Easter Season, or during the fifty days of the Easter Season. It is most appropriate as a guide through the Rite of Christian Initiation of Adults' period of post-baptismal catechesis or mystagogy with the newly baptized during the Easter Season, especially with its emphasis on spiritual growth through prayer. It can also be used during a retreat or on days set aside for reflection. Small groups of people might use it, reading its entries, sharing their reflections, and closing with its concluding prayer.

The book is designed to help the reader grow in prayer based on the example of Jesus in Luke's Gospel and based on the example of the apostles in the Acts of the Apostles. This author hopes that those who pray their way through Luke's Gospel and the Acts of the Apostles will become better pray-ers.

Mark G. Boyer
April 25, 2015
Feast of St. Mark, Evangelist

PART 1

Prayer in Luke's Gospel

PEOPLE AT PRAYER
(1:10): December 19; June 24 (Vigil)

Scripture: ". . . At the time of the incense offering, the whole assembly of the people was praying outside [the sanctuary of the Lord]." (Luke 1:10)

Reflection: The first mention of prayer in Luke's Gospel is found with the act of burning incense. An incense offering to God is made in the morning and the evening according to the LORD's directive to Moses (cf. Exod 30:7–8). Fragrant incense not only pleases God's nose, but it serves as a sacrifice that is turned into smoke by fire and rises up to the heaven, above which God lives.

Sometimes called frankincense, incense is a resin produced by a family of desert trees that grow in southern Arabia. It is derived from a sap that dries, forming crystalline lumps of an amber/gold color. Often other gums and spices are added to it to enrich its pleasing fragrance.

Part 1

The Jews regarded its rich spicy scent as a pure offering, pleasing to God, but even earlier than the Israelites incense was used in Egypt, Greece, and Rome as a way to honor gods and as a medicine and a base for perfume.

The burning of incense represents zeal and fervor. Its fragrance represents virtue. Its rising smoke represents acceptable prayer, as noted in Psalm 141:2: "Let my prayer be counted as incense before you, [O LORD,] and the lifting up of my hands as an evening sacrifice."

Thus, the author of Luke's Gospel portrays the whole assembly of people at prayer while Zechariah the priest offers the evening incense. Luke understands there to be a group of Jews who were expectant of God's coming to set them free from Roman oppression. Zechariah's offering of incense inside the sanctuary serves as an aid to their prayer outside.

Incense can still serve as an aid to prayer. Today it comes as sticks and powders and candles and can be burned in a variety of ways. Its many available fragrances gives the pray-er choices as to how he or she will stimulate his or her olfactory sense. Some people become too focused on prayer as saying words; incense stimulates another bodily sense and draws one into prayer through smell. According to Luke's Gospel, it brought the assembly of the people into prayer while Zechariah was offering it in the sanctuary; it can bring both assemblies of people and individuals into prayer, into God's presence today.

Meditation: Have you ever used incense to pray? If you have, what do you remember about that time of prayer? If you have not, entertain the idea of buying some incense and burning it to draw you into prayer. Have you ever been a member of an assembly that used incense for prayer? What do you remember about that experience of prayer?

Prayer: LORD God, let my prayer rise up to you like burning incense. Make me acceptable in your sight, and grant that my offering be pleasing to you, who live and reign as Father, Son, and Holy Spirit, three persons, yet one God, forever and ever. Amen.

Prayer in Luke's Gospel
ZECHARIAH AT PRAYER
(1:11–13): December 19; June 24 (Vigil)

Scripture: ". . . [T]here appeared to [Zechariah] an angel of the Lord, standing at the right side of the altar of incense. When Zechariah saw him, he was terrified; and fear overwhelmed him. But the angel said to him, 'Do not be afraid, Zechariah, for your prayer has been heard. Your wife Elizabeth will bear you a son, and you will name him John.'" (Luke 1:11–13)

Reflection: Using a favorite Hebrew Bible (Old Testament) name for God's messenger—angel of the Lord—Luke uniquely presents a priest named Zechariah experiencing divine revelation at the time he was burning incense in the Temple in the evening. There is no description given of the angel of the Lord, but Zechariah's response is typical of others in the Bible who have been direct recipients of divine revelation: fear.

Fear is a sign of wisdom. Once Zechariah has demonstrated his wisdom, the angel—whom the reader later finds out is named Gabriel, meaning "God's strength"—calms the priest's fear and tells him that his prayer has been heard by God and is about to be answered. Zechariah and Elizabeth are elderly, "living blamelessly according to all the commandments and regulations of the Lord" (1:6), but childless. So, their prayer has been for God to give them a child. In other words, God's strength is stronger than human strength when it comes to procreation.

An astute reader will recognize the Hebrew Bible (Old Testament) prototype for this story as Abraham and Sarah, who, both being elderly and obedient to God, are childless even though the LORD keeps telling them that they will be the parents of a nation that is as numerous as the stars of the sky or the sands on the seashore. They trust God's promise and conceive Isaac. Likewise, Zechariah and Elizabeth will conceive John the Baptizer, who like Isaac, will be great in the sight of the Lord.

This account of Zechariah's visitation by Gabriel confirms that prayers are heard by God. The story also confirms that prayer is also listening to God speak through his messengers, be they angels or otherwise.

Meditation: Identify a recent experience of prayer that involved you both talking to God and listening to his response. For what/whom were you praying? What response did you get?

Prayer: All-holy God, you heard the prayer of Zechariah and Elizabeth for a child in their older years. Graciously hear my prayers, and mercifully give me ears open to hear your response. I ask this through your Son, Jesus Christ, who lives and reigns with you and the Holy Spirit, one God, forever and ever. Amen.

ANNA AT PRAYER

(2:36–38): December 30; February 2

Scripture: "There was . . . a prophet[ess] Anna . . . . She was of a great age, having lived with her husband seven years after her marriage, then as a widow to the age of eighty-four. She never left the temple but worshiped there with fasting and prayer night and day. . . . [S]he came, and began to praise God and to speak about the child [Jesus] to all who were looking for the redemption of Jerusalem." (Luke 2:36–38)

Reflection: In another uniquely Lukan narrative, the reader encounters the prophet(ess) Anna as the infant Jesus is brought to the Jerusalem Temple to be presented to the Lord. The first to see and comment upon the fate of the child is Simeon; the second to do so is Anna. This story illustrates a characteristic of the author of Luke's Gospel, namely, that after narrating an account about a man, he will often narrate one about a woman, or vice-versa.

Anna, like Simeon before her, is a prophet(ess), one who speaks for God about a current situation and offers hope to those who listen to the speaker's words. Eighty-four-year-old Anna worships in the Temple. She fasts, meaning she empties herself so that she can receive God's revelation. She prays day and night, meaning she speaks to God and listens to his reply. Anna fulfills her role as a prophet(ess) by speaking about the infant Jesus to all who are looking for the redemption of Jerusalem, namely, its liberation from Roman occupation forces.

Anna's prototype is the Old Testament (Apocrypha) Judith. After displaying bravery equal to any man, Judith saves her village and, ultimately, Jerusalem from Holofernes, the chief general of the army of Nebuchadnezzar, king of the Assyrians. Once her husband dies, she spends her widowhood dressed in sackcloth and fasting. Like Anna, she gives thanks to God for the redemption of the land, that is, its liberation from Assyrian forces.

The story of Anna reminds the reader that prayer precedes one speaking for God about a current situation and offering hope to those who listen to the speaker's words. Hope grows out of prayer, which is nourished by fasting. Before one can be filled with God's word, one must first be emptied in preparation to receive it. In a culture that oftentimes fasts from nothing—and always fosters being filled—Anna's story serves as a Christian antidote.

Meditation: Identify a recent experience of prayer that was preceded by fasting. How empty were you of food, noise, activity, etc.? With what word of God were you filled?

Prayer: Almighty God, through the mouths of your prophets you speak your word. Give me the strength to fast, so that I may be a worthy recipient of your Word, Jesus Christ, who sets me free from sin and fills me with your grace. You are one God—Father, Son, and Holy Spirit—forever and ever. Amen.

JESUS AT PRAYER

(3:21–22): The Baptism of the Lord, Cycle C

Scripture: "Now when all the people were baptized, and when Jesus also had been baptized and was praying, the heaven was opened, and the Holy Spirit descended upon him in bodily form

Part 1

like a dove. And a voice came from heaven, 'You are my Son, the Beloved; with you I am well pleased.'" (Luke 3:21–22)

Reflection: The first time Luke portrays Jesus at prayer is at his baptism. Unique to the Lukan account of Jesus' baptism is the notice that John the Baptist was locked in prison by Herod Antipas before Jesus was baptized (cf. 3:19–20). With John removed from the account, the focus is on Jesus alone and his baptism by the Holy Spirit.

Luke, who is the first evangelist to develop a theology of the Spirit, prepares the reader for this scene with the earlier account of Jesus' conception. Gabriel tells Mary, "The Holy Spirit will come upon you, and the power of the Most High will overshadow you; therefore the child to be born will be holy; he will be called Son of God" (1:35). In Luke's understanding, Jesus is a Spirit-child. The baptism narrative confirms this.

The Holy Spirit descends from the opened heaven, where ancient people thought God lived, to the earth, where people lived. And like the Spirit of the LORD once confirmed the anointing of both Saul and David as king of Israel, the Holy Spirit now confirms Jesus as the Messiah, the Hebrew word for "anointed," indicating that he is the chosen one of God.

Even the divine voice echoes a phrase from a royal psalm most likely used during the coronation of Judean kings: "You are my son" (Psalm 2:7), combined with a phrase from the first suffering servant poem in Isaiah which introduces the royal emissary at court: "Here is . . . my chosen, in whom my soul delights" (42:1). Thus, Jesus, who was first introduced to Mary through her conception of him by the Holy Spirit, is now introduced to the whole world by the same Holy Spirit at his baptism.

All this takes place while Jesus is praying. Prayer opens the follower of Jesus to the Holy Spirit. Prayer sets the stage for a breakthrough from heaven. A person most likely will not see a dove, but maybe feel a gentle breeze, a few rays of sun on the skin, or a raindrop or two falling on the forehead. Maybe a deep breath awakens one to the Holy Spirit, who claims people for God and introduces them to their mission through baptism.

Meditation: Recently, when have you been praying and experienced the Holy Spirit in some bodily form introducing you to your next mission?

Prayer: At his baptism in the Jordan River, O LORD, you anointed your Son, the Beloved, with the Holy Spirit. Pour that same Spirit upon me, that I may know my mission, fully embrace it, and be pleasing in your sight. I ask this in the name of Jesus Christ, who lives and reigns with you and the Holy Spirit, one God, forever and ever. Amen.

DESERT PRAYER

(5:15–16): Friday after Epiphany or January 11

Scripture: "... [N]ow more than ever the word about Jesus spread abroad; many crowds would gather to hear him and to be cured of their diseases. But he would withdraw to deserted places and pray." (Luke 5:15–16)

Reflection: Because most people participate in all types of social networks and gatherings and spend most of their time with others, going to the desert is not very high on their list of places to visit. Most likely, it is not on their list at all! In other words, the desert does not draw modern people to itself.

However, the isolation of the desert as a perfect place to pray is a theme found throughout the Bible. Once Moses leads the Hebrews out of Egypt, he takes them to the desert, where they are formed into God's people. Many of the prophets spent a lot of time in the desert, listening to God tell them what message they needed to deliver to his people. Therefore, the author of Luke's Gospel aptly portrays Jesus going to the desert to pray, especially after teaching and healing. In the desert, Jesus, spiritually spent from teaching and healing, could reconnect with God and rejuvenate his spirit for the next step of his journey.

One doesn't have to go to a literal desert in order to have a desert experience. A desert can be created in an upstairs room, in a basement, or in the back yard. Desert requirements are minimal. The place needs to be free from distractions—no computer, no cell phone, no TV, no radio. Food and water are minimal. Silence is required. Other people are informed that they need to stay away.

While sitting, standing, or walking in the desert retreat, one becomes aware that he or she is surrounded by God's life-giving presence; one enters into a womb whose amniotic fluid is Spirit. The human spiritual umbilical cord is connected to God, and the result is rebirth in prayer and spiritual rejuvenation.

Jesus went often to the desert to pray. Like him, modern people need to create or find a desert in which they can be spiritually nourished for their life's work.

Meditation: Where is your desert? What kinds of spiritual rebirth have occurred there?

Prayer: Ever-living God, you draw your people to the desert so that you can nourish their spirits. Lead me to a place where I can reconnect my spirit with your life-giving Spirit. I ask this in the name of Jesus Christ, who himself went often to the desert to pray; he lives and reigns with you and the Holy Spirit, one God, forever and ever. Amen.

DISCERNMENT PRAYER

(6:12–13): Tuesday of the Twenty-Third Week in Ordinary Time, Years I & II; October 28

Scripture: "Now during those days [Jesus] went out to the mountain to pray; and he spent the night in prayer to God. And when day came, he called his disciples and chose twelve of them, whom he also named apostles . . . ." (Luke 6:12–13)

Prayer in Luke's Gospel

Reflection: Jesus has choices to make. Like Jacob's twelve sons are the foundation stones for the nation of Israel, Jesus will choose twelve apostles from many disciples to serve as the foundation for what the author of Luke's Gospel understands to be the new Israel, what modern people know as Christianity. Before making his choices, Jesus spends time in discernment prayer.

He begins his prayer by going to an unnamed mountain. In the ancient world's cosmology, the earth was the center of the universe, and it was composed of three stories or levels. There was the underworld or netherworld, where the dead lived. There was the flat, plate-like surface, where people lived. And there was the heaven, above which God lived. So, by going to a mountain to pray Jesus gets as close to God as he can while still remaining on earth.

He spends the night in prayer. In later Christian history, this becomes known as a vigil, staying awake all night in prayer in preparation for a feast or some other important event. Jesus keeps vigil and discerns which twelve of his disciples he will choose as apostles. While maintaining wakefulness, he discerns or comes to know the will of God. Implied in the process of discernment prayer is a naming and separation of the human will from God's will and a desire to do God's will.

Based on a presupposition that God directs people through the experiences of their lives, discernment prayer is often set within the context of evaluating the senses. For example, what does one know about all the choices from which one has to choose? How does one feel about each of the choices? What does each of the choices taste like? smell like? sound like? Is there a biblical story that might help inform one's choices? The pray-er believes that through such critical reflection, God's will is revealed.

Luke presents Jesus as model of discernment prayer. While he does not tell the reader what Jesus thought or what he may have said to God, the act of Jesus going to a mountain and spending the night in discernment prayer indicates that before important choices it is a good practice to seek God's will. In other words, at the major turning points in the reader's life, such as a choice of a college major, vocation, job, etc., a good practice is discernment prayer.

Meditation: What major turning point are you getting ready to face? From what choices must you choose? What do you know about each choice? feel about each choice? What does each choice taste like? smell like? sound like? What similar biblical story may inform your choice?

Prayer: Ever-speaking God, you whisper your words in the depths of my heart. With the aid of the Holy Spirit, help me to discern your will for my life. Then, give me the courage to follow through with my decision. Hear my prayer through Jesus Christ, your Son, who lives and reigns with you and the Holy Spirit, one God, forever and ever. Amen.

PRAYER FOR ADVERSARIES

(6:20, 27–28): Sixth Sunday in Ordinary Time, Cycle C; Wednesday of the Twenty-Third Week in Ordinary Time, Years I & II; Thursday of the Twenty-Third Week in Ordinary Time, Years I & II; November 17; December 23

Scripture: Jesus ". . . looked up at his disciples and said: . . . 'Love your enemies, do good to those who hate you, bless those who curse you, pray for those who abuse you.'" (Luke 6:20, 27–28)

Reflection: After Jesus chooses twelve apostles, those who will be sent with his message, he comes down the mountain and begins to teach a great multitude of people, including apostles and disciples. In the course of his instructing, he teaches them four aspects of what can only be called radical discipleship.

First, followers of Jesus are to love their enemies. This oxymoronic statement refers to an attitude rather than an emotion. It is best understood as desiring the good of others, even those whom one considers to be his or her enemy. Second, Jesus instructs his followers to do good to those who hate them. Instead of countering hate with hate, disciples are to replace hate with good. Instead of adding to a division between "them" and "us," disciples are to heal the division created by another by doing good. Third, actions now turn to words. Instead of cursing, that is, wishing evil upon one who curses another, Jesus' followers bless them. And, fourth, those who wear the name of disciple pray for those who abuse them, that is, verbally reproach or scorn them for their way of life.

The prayer for adversaries begins with a change in one's attitude—from hate to love—and progresses to speech—from curse to blessing—and finishes with action—from retaliation to going beyond what is usually required. Praying for one's adversaries is, indeed, going beyond; it demonstrates radical discipleship.

Later in Luke's Gospel, Jesus will practice these four aspects of radical discipleship. Before he dies on the cross he declares his love for his enemies; he will do good for those who hate him; he will bless those who have betrayed him; and he will pray for those who have crucified him. Those who call themselves disciples of Jesus—Christians—learn the prayer for adversaries from the One they follow.

Reflection: Choose an adversary and decide to love him or her. What good can you do for him or her? What blessing, wishing good, can you ask for him or her? What prayer can you say for the person?

Prayer: Mighty God, your Son, Jesus Christ, has taught me to love all people the way you love them and to desire their good the way you desire it. Through your grace, cause a blessing and prayer for my adversaries to well up in me, that I may be a follower in word and deed of the same Jesus Christ, my Lord, who lives and reigns with you and the Holy Spirit, one God, forever and ever. Amen.

Part 1

FASTING AND PRAYER

(6:33–35): Seventh Sunday in Ordinary Time, Cycle C; Thursday of the Twenty-Third Week in Ordinary Time, Years I & II; November 17; December 23

Scripture: "[The Pharisees and their scribes said to Jesus,] 'John's disciples, like the disciples of the Pharisees, frequently fast and pray, but your disciples eat and drink.' Jesus said to them, 'You cannot make wedding guests fast while the bridegroom is with them, can you? The days will come when the bridegroom will be taken away from them, and then they will fast in those days.'" (Luke 6:33–35)

Reflection: There is a connection between fasting and praying as indicated in part of the dialogue between Jesus and the Pharisees and their scribes in the home of the tax collector named Levi. The connection between fasting and praying is attributed to the disciples of John the Baptist who, like the disciples of the Pharisees, both fasted and prayed. Fasting and prayer are an important aspect of Jewish piety, and both are understood by the author of Luke-Acts to be important aspects of Christian piety as well.

Fasting, the act of choosing to abstain from food or from some food, empties a person and sparks hunger pangs and a growling stomach. One cannot be filled unless he or she is first emptied. Thus, fasting prepares one for prayer, for communion with God. Furthermore, the hunger that results from eating nothing or sparingly reminds the pray-er of his or her hunger for God; it is a hunger for the divine that only God can satisfy.

In the Christian tradition, as reflected in Luke's Gospel, fasting and prayer were associated with waiting for Christ's return in glory. The wedding feast was a metaphor employed by the prophets to describe what the union of God, the bridegroom, and the people as a collective, the bride, would be like. Luke reinterprets the metaphor, declaring Jesus to be the new bridegroom who, while he is with his people, does not urge his disciple to fast and pray. However, once he dies, is raised, and ascends into heaven, then his disciples will fast and pray while they await his return.

Prayer in Luke's Gospel

Many people are familiar with fasting and prayer during the liturgical season of Lent, but may not practice it outside of those forty days. Fasting from all or some food for a predetermined length of time and/or abstaining from certain food, like meat, for a predetermined length of time empties and cleanses the fast-er and prepares him or her to enter into a prayer that is best characterized as a deep-felt hunger for God. Fasting and prayer can also awaken the fast-er to his or her dependence for life—and the food that nourishes life—on God and the return of his Son in glory. The bride awaits the groom, who will satisfy her every hunger.

Meditation: What combination of fasting and prayer have you experienced? How did fasting enable a deeper prayer hunger for you? How did God satisfy your hunger?

Prayer: God of all life, you provide for all you have created. Through my fasting, empty me of everything that cannot satisfy, so that through the prayer you inspire, I may hunger for you alone and be filled with your grace as I wait in joyful hope for the coming of Jesus Christ, your Son, who lives and reigns with you and the Holy Spirit, one God, forever and ever. Amen.

PRAYER ALONE

(9:18): Twelfth Sunday in Ordinary Time, Cycle C; Friday of the Twenty-Fifth Week in Ordinary Time, Years I & II

Scripture: "Once when Jesus was praying alone, with only the disciples near him, he asked them, 'Who do the crowds say that I am?'" (Luke 9:18)

Reflection: Many people have abandoned private prayer or prayer alone in favor of public prayer or prayer with others. Unless there is a group, singing and saying words together, no praying is done by many people. While both private prayer and public prayer enhance each other and lead the pray-er from one to the next and

Part 1

back again, the Lukan Jesus often demonstrates the importance of prayer alone that is, indeed, prayer with others.

Praying privately does not exclude Jesus' disciples. Luke notes that they were near him enough for him to ask them a question about what identity others are giving him. After the disciples report what they have heard, Jesus asks them, "But who do you say that I am?" (9:20) Peter answers, "The Messiah of God" (9:20). Peter's response is meant to echo for the reader the account of the angel of the Lord's words to the shepherds, ". . . [T]o you is born this day in the city of David a Savior, who is the Messiah, the Lord" (2:11), and the narrator's description of Simeon as one to whom "it had been revealed . . . by the Holy Spirit that he would not see death before he had seen the Lord's Messiah" (2:26).

Messiah is a Hebrew word meaning "anointed." Likewise, Christ is a Greek word meaning "anointed." Thus, Peter's declaration that Jesus is God's anointed indicates that God has chosen Jesus, like God chose the past kings of Judah, to complete a mission that only he can accomplish. It is while praying alone that the question wells up in Jesus and is spoken to his disciples. It is while praying alone that he hears God's answer spoken and confirmed through Peter's lips. Jesus' identity as Messiah will be the charge for his execution later in the story.

Prayer alone is being in the presence of God and in communion with him. Through this simple act, one's identity is revealed and may be confirmed by others who may be praying near one. One's communion with God is simultaneously communion with others who are in prayer alone. In other words, prayer alone does not automatically exclude prayer with others. In fact, the best prayer with others may be prayer alone, as demonstrated by Jesus.

Meditation: Recall a recent experience of praying alone. What presence of God did you discover? What presence of others did you discover?

Prayer: Ever-present God, make me aware of your presence as I enter into this prayer alone. Through the power of the Holy Spirit, unite me to all others who are in communion with you. May I come to know better my own identity as a member of the body of Christ, your Son, who lives and reigns with you and the Holy Spirit, one God, forever and ever. Amen.

TRANSFIGURING PRAYER
(9:28–29): Second Sunday of Lent, Cycle C; August 6, Cycle C

Scripture: "Now about eight days after these sayings Jesus took with him Peter and John and James, and went up on the mountain to pray. And while he was praying, the appearance of his face changed, and his clothes became dazzling white." (Luke 9:28–29)

Reflection: After teaching discipleship, Jesus goes up a mountain to pray and experiences an epiphany, a divine appearance, similar to the epiphany at his baptism. All the biblical signs for an epiphany are given. The scene is set eight days later than Jesus' teaching; eight is a biblical number indicating completeness. The account contains three sets of three—three apostles: Peter, James, John; three other men of whom two have been long dead and one who will be dead soon: Moses, Elijah, Jesus; and three dwellings or tents. Three signifies the spiritual order. And the cloud with the voice coming from it and declaring, "This is my Son, my Chosen; listen to him" (9:35), like the voice from heaven at Jesus' baptism, indicates that God is revealing himself.

Luke's unique report of this scene explains that while Jesus is praying, he is transfigured, that is, his face changes and his clothes become dazzlingly white. Maybe this scene is best described by saying that Jesus became transparent, and God's light shone through him. This divine light also brings to the stage two other men who were thought to have been transparent to God. Moses, who, like Jesus, often communed with God on a mountain, was thought to have known the LORD face to face. Elijah, who, again like Jesus, often communed with God on a mountain, was thought to have entered above the heaven, where God lives, in a fiery chariot.

Furthermore, Moses represents the law, and Elijah represents the prophets. Jesus, who unites these in himself to create a new

Part 1

Israel, will die and be raised in Jerusalem, from where he will also depart in the unique Lukan account of the ascension. Before all this takes place, however, Jesus, like Moses, who anointed Joshua with the Spirit as his successor, and Elijah, who anointed Elisha with the Spirit as his successor, will bestow upon his apostles the Holy Spirit.

Prayer can change the pray-er. Truly entering into the presence of God without a plan of what God needs to do leaves the pray-er vulnerable to change or transfiguration. Total openness to God's will for one provides God with the opportunity to shape or mold the person in such a way that he or she becomes transparent, like a window through whom God's light shines.

Transfiguring prayer is grounded in faith, absolute trust in God. Faith, adherence to God beyond what can be either sensed or understood, is the foundation for this prayer that God prays in people, who become instruments of God's will and vehicles of God's light. Transfiguring prayer is not brought about by the pray-er; transfiguring prayer is the prayer that God prays in him or her, making the person transparent so that God's glory—already shared by Moses and Elijah—is manifest. The transfiguration of Jesus is an epiphany of the LORD's glory; it is also a glimpse of the LORD's glory that will be revealed later in the gospel through Jesus' resurrection and ascension into heaven.

Meditation: Recall a recent experience of God praying in you. What changes occurred in you? How did you experience transparency? How were you a means for God to manifest himself to the world?

Prayer: On the mountain while he was praying, you revealed your glory, God of Light, through your Son, Jesus Christ. Instill in me an absolute faith like his, that I may be your willing and transparent servant through whom you manifest your presence. One day I hope to share in the fullness of the glory you share as Father, Son, and Holy Spirit, one God, forever and ever. Amen.

Prayer in Luke's Gospel

JESUS' PRAYER

(10:21–22) Tuesday of the First Week of Advent, Years I & II

Scripture: "... Jesus rejoiced in the Holy Spirit and said, 'I thank you, Father, Lord of heaven and earth, because you have hidden these things from the wise and the intelligent and have revealed them to infants; yes, Father, for such was your gracious will. All things have been handed over to me by my Father; and no one knows who the Son is except the Father, or who the Father is except the Son and anyone to whom the Son chooses to reveal him.'" (Luke 10:21–22)

Reflection: Luke records one of the few actual prayers we have that Jesus may have said following the unique account of Jesus appointing seventy (or seventy-two) other disciples in pairs as missionaries to all the places he intended to visit and their return to report to Jesus what they accomplished in his name. "At that same hour Jesus rejoiced in the Holy Spirit . . ." (10:21). As one conceived by the Holy Spirit, Jesus' prayer illustrates the Lukan theme that the presence of the Spirit is a sign of the coming of the kingdom of God. Through his words and deeds, Jesus brings that kingdom into the world; he spreads the Spirit everywhere.

Under the influence of the Spirit, Jesus begins his prayer with thanksgiving to the Father, who is Lord or King of heaven and earth. As such, it follows a pattern of Jewish prayer in synagogues. After the thanksgiving Jesus acknowledges God's power and God's way, neither of which conform to the power or way of the world. God hides things from the wise and the intelligent; the world worships the wise and intelligent. God reveals things to infants; the world doesn't think infants know anything. However, this is God's will; this is God's way of bringing about his kingdom through the Holy Spirit at work in Jesus.

God has entrusted all things to his Son. In other words, Jesus has been given all stewardship of the kingdom. This is why Luke's Gospel is unique when Jesus declares to the Pharisees, "... [T]he kingdom of God is among you" (17:21). It is among them in the person of the Father's Son, Jesus. Some translations state that it is "within" them; because the kingdom is influenced by the Holy Spirit, who permeates all things, it is within also.

The Son of God and God have a unique relationship according to Jesus' prayer. Only the Father knows exactly who the Son is, and only the Son knows exactly who the Father is. This type of relational language is very Johannine; it is not found frequently in the gospels of Mark, Matthew, or Luke. Because Jesus has been entrusted with the stewardship of the Father's kingdom through the working of the Holy Spirit, he can reveal the Father to whomever he chooses. In making the kingdom present, Jesus reveals the Father to those who are ready to recognize and receive it.

Among those who are ready to recognize and receive it are Jesus' disciples. As soon as he finishes his prayer, he turns to them privately and declares them blessed because they see what prophets and kings longed to see, but did not see; they hear what prophets and kings longed to hear, but did not hear, namely, the kingdom of God among them. The prayer has now come full circle. The disciples are the infants to whom God has revealed his kingdom; the prophets and the kings are the intelligent and wise from whom God has hidden it.

God's kingdom is among all, but it goes unnoticed because most people are not seeing where it is or hearing where it is. It is sought in the words of the intelligent and wise in lectures, articles, and books, but it is seen in the faces of infants and heard in their babble. The Father's rule has been entrusted to his Son, Jesus, who, under the influence of the Spirit, makes it present in his words and deeds for those who can hear and see.

Meditation: If you open your eyes wide, where do you see God's kingdom coming? If you listen intently with your ears, where do you hear good news of God's kingdom coming? Keep in mind that it cannot be seen in the usual way of seeing, and it cannot be heard in the usual way of hearing. Seeing and hearing the kingdom begin under the influence of the Holy Spirit.

Prayer in Luke's Gospel

Prayer: Father, Lord of heaven and earth, your gracious will is to reveal your kingdom to infants. Send your Holy Spirit to me, that I might see with the eyes of an infant and hear with the ears of an infant what your Son has revealed to the world: that your kingdom is here. Knowing this, may I know you, Father, and your Son, Jesus Christ, and your Holy Spirit, who live and reign as one God, forever and ever. Amen.

PRAYING PRAYER

(11:1–2): Seventeenth Sunday in Ordinary Time, Cycle C; Wednesday of the Twenty-Seventh Week in Ordinary Time, Years I & II

Scripture: "[Jesus] was praying in a certain place, and after he had finished, one of his disciples said, 'Lord, teach us to pray, as John taught his disciples.' He said to them, 'When you pray, say: Father, hallowed be your name. Your kingdom come.'" (Luke 11:1–2)

Reflection: The fact that Jesus is found praying, before he teaches his disciple to pray, signals that this is an important scene in Luke's Gospel. The author emphasizes critical scenes in Jesus' ministry by portraying him at prayer. Here, Luke portrays Jesus as a master pray-er, teaching his followers his method.

A place is chosen. Often it is a mountain. Sometimes it is another place. For the human person place often indicates function. No one would debate that the place called church or synagogue or mosque or temple is associated primarily with prayer. Some people prepare a prayer corner in a room or a prayer room or a chapel and decorate it with items associated with prayer, such as a Bible, a candle, a cross, etc.

Before the master pray-er begins to teach prayer, he himself prays. In other words, as Jesus prays, he teaches prayer. The form of the Lord's Prayer preserved in Luke's Gospel indicates that it begins by addressing God as a child would call his or her parents: Father. Then, the pray-er sanctifies God's name, a typical feature of

Jewish prayer, before expressing a desire that God's rule be made effective in the world.

The petition for daily bread emphasizes the dependency of the pray-er on God, who created all things and, thus, owns all things and allots portions as they are needed. The next petition may be the most radical of the prayer; it asks God to forgive sins as sinners forgive each other. In other words, there is a condition placed upon this request. The pray-er asks to be forgiven to the same degree that he or she forgives others.

The final petition, asking God not to bring the pray-er to the time of trial, reflects a biblical presupposition that God is in control of the world and all that goes on in it. Thus, if a time of trial comes, it is understood to be a test from God, much like Abraham was tested to offer Isaac as a sacrifice to God.

The five-step method of prayer taught by Jesus in Luke's Gospel is not the only version of the Lord's Prayer, although it is the simplest. There is a seven-step version in Matthew's Gospel, a version in an early church document called *The Didache* that follows Matthew's version but adds a doxology, and the version memorized by most Christians and recited together during group and private prayer.

As is the case with many printed and/or memorized prayers, the Lord's Prayer easily can become rote recitation. The pray-er may want to consider the example of Jesus, who prays before he teaches prayer; he is one who prays prayer.

Meditation: What has been your experience with the Lord's Prayer? Do you pray it or recite it from memory? Have you used the other versions of it? Is your place for prayer conducive to praying prayer?

Prayer: Father, I praise your name beyond all names. Grant me the grace to submit myself to the rule of your kingdom, in which I depend upon you for food, forgiveness, and peace. These petitions come before you through my Lord, Jesus Christ, who lives and reigns with you and the Holy Spirit, one God, forever and ever. Amen.

Prayer in Luke's Gospel

PRAY ALWAYS

(18:1, 6–8): Twenty-Ninth Sunday in Ordinary Time, Cycle C; Saturday of the Thirty-Second Week in Ordinary Time, Years I & II

Scripture: ". . . Jesus told [his disciples] a parable about their need to pray always and not to lose heart. And the Lord said, '. . . Will not God grant justice to his chosen ones who cry to him day and night? Will he delay long in helping them? I tell you, he will quickly grant justice to them.'" (Luke 18:1, 6–8)

Reflection: Praying always does not imply perpetual prayer, but as the parable Jesus tells illustrates consistency and perseverance even in the face of great difficulty. The story is about a judge who neither fears God nor respects people. A widow, that is, a disenfranchised person because she has no man to plead her cause, has a case pending before the judge. She continues to appear before the judge, demanding justice. For a while he ignores her, but finally, getting tired of her pestering him, he rules in her favor.

The widow is the model for one to pray always. She consistently appeared before the judge, seeking justice. She did not give up when he did not adjudicate her case. Finally, in order to get rid of her, he gives her what she wants. Her persistence and perseverance get her a favorable answer to her case.

As is typical for many parables in Luke's Gospel, the author provides an introduction and a conclusion which illustrates Luke's intended meaning of the parable. The opening line serves as a bookend for the parable, indicating that it illustrates characteristics about prayer. The closing verses serve as the other bookend for the story, illustrating that God grants what is due to those who call out to him day and night, that is, who pray always. God does not delay in answering them; he acts upon their request quickly. Indeed, God is not like the judge who only acts to avoid the widow's pestering; God acts with mercy.

Thus, while the narrative is about the need to pray always consistently and persistently, it is also about the God who answers prayers without delay because he is merciful. Knowing this enables the pray-er to trust God. If an unjust judge will grant a widow's plea for justice, how much more will God grant the prayers of those who pray always? God is not only trustworthy; God is also faithful and merciful when faced with prayer both day and night.

Meditation: What has been your recent experience of praying day and night? Did your praying always develop a deeper trust in God? Did you come to know God's faithfulness and mercy in ways you never knew them before?

Prayer: Ever-present and all-knowing God, you never cease to hear those who cry out to you day and night. In your mercy, strengthen my faith and keep me close to you so that I do not lose heart. Hear my prayer through your Son, Jesus Christ, who taught me to pray always in the Holy Spirit, who lives and reigns with you, Father, as one God, forever and ever. Amen.

PRAYER STANCE

(18:10–11, 13–14): Thirtieth Sunday in Ordinary Time, Cycle C; Saturday of the Third Week of Lent, Years I & II

Scripture: Jesus told this parable: "Two men went up to the temple to pray, one a Pharisee and the other tax collector. The Pharisee, standing by himself, was praying thus, 'God, I thank you that I am not like other people: thieves, rogues, adulterers, or even like this tax collector.' But the tax collector, standing far off, would not even look up to heaven, but was beating his breast and saying, 'God, be merciful to me, a sinner.' I tell you, this man went down to his home justified rather than the other . . . ." (Luke 18:10–11, 13–14)

Reflection: There are two ways to understand "prayer stance." The first is in terms of physical posture. Both men, who went to the temple to pray in the parable, take the physical position of standing. The second way to understand "prayer stance" is in terms of mental attitude or mental presupposition.

Prayer in Luke's Gospel

Throughout Luke's Gospel and the Acts of the Apostles, the temple is portrayed as a place of prayer. Later in the gospel, Jesus will cleanse the temple of all that is not prayer. It is the attitude or mental presupposition that gives the parable its power. The Pharisee, representing a composite of all Pharisees, has been portrayed throughout the gospel as rejecting God's will and justifying himself, whereas the tax collector, again representing a composite of all tax collectors and sinners, has been portrayed as open to Jesus' words and conversion.

Furthermore, in the context of the story, the Pharisee is a leader of Judaism. After the return from Babylonian exile, the sect of the Pharisees became the teachers of the Torah or Law. They are the dominant group—among such others as Sadducees and Essenes—representing strict observance of the written Torah and their oral interpretation of it. Simply put, the Pharisee is a good man.

The tax collector, however, represents the outcast. He is despised because he works for the Roman occupation government. He makes his living by raising the set amount of the Roman tax and pocketing the difference. Thus, not only does he work for the enemy, but he makes his living off of his fellow Jews. There is no doubt that he is a bad man.

The Pharisee stands and prays by himself. It is very difficult to translate this sentence from the Greek into English because there are too many connotations that no one English phrase can capture. The phrase means that the Pharisee prayed to himself, that he prayed quietly to himself, that he prayed to himself rather than to God, and that he prayed with reference to himself. Thus, even though he addresses "God" in his prayer, it is a prayer to himself, indicating that he is not dependent upon God.

This becomes clear in his prayer. He thanks God that he is not like other people; he is an elitist. Basically, his prayer is telling God what he, the Pharisee, has done. Thus, he is better than other people because he is not a thief, a rogue, an adulterer, or a tax collector. Furthermore, he fasts twice a week and tithes a tenth of his income. He is boasting that his practices go beyond the legal requirements. His says his prayer while seeing the despised tax collector out of the corner of his eye.

The tax collector knows his place as a sinner in God's world. He stands far off, not daring to come close to the LORD, who is all-holy. He does not even dare to raise his eyes; he does not look up towards God nor does he see the Pharisee. He is totally dependent upon God's mercy, demonstrating this through the beating of his breast, a sign of repentance.

The original hearer's conclusion would have been that the Pharisee was justified in God's eyes, and the tax collector was unrighteous. However, that is not how Jesus ends the story. The places are reversed. The tax collector is justified by God, that is, God considers him to be righteous or acceptable to God, whereas the Pharisee is not.

The parable teaches that one's prayer stance cannot be an attitude of power. One does not enter into prayer from a position of power, like the Pharisee, but from a presupposition of powerlessness, like the tax collector. Furthermore, honest self-knowledge is required. The Pharisee didn't know himself; he merely presumed that his stance or place in the world confirmed his justification. The tax collector knew himself; he presumed nothing except the hoped-for mercy of God.

Meditation: What is your experience of praying like a Pharisee? What is your experience of praying like a tax collector? In what ways does the parable remind you that prayer is not about you, but about God?

Prayer: O God, you hear the prayer of those who seek your forgiveness. Have mercy on me, a sinner. I have sinned through my fault in thoughts and deeds and in what I have done and failed to do. Justify me through your Son, Jesus Christ, who lives and reigns with you and the Holy Spirit, one God, forever and ever. Amen.

Prayer in Luke's Gospel
HOUSE OF PRAYER
(19:45–46): Friday of the Thirty-Third Week in Ordinary Time, Years I & II

Scripture: Jesus "entered the temple and began to drive out those who were selling things there; and he said, 'It is written, "My house shall be a house of prayer"; but you have made it a den of robbers.'" (Luke 19:45–46)

Reflection: This visit of Jesus to the temple is his first since he sat among the teachers, listening to them and asking them questions when he was a twelve-year-old boy. In order to prepare to demonstrate his teaching ability again, he needs first to cleanse the temple of all that is not prayer.

By the time of Jesus, the temple had become a marketplace, where pilgrims could buy animals for sacrifice, pay their temple tax, and pay any other expenses, especially the cost of changing money. Jesus casts out all such activity, that is, he exorcises the temple of the evil profanation he finds there. Quoting a phrase from Isaiah 56:7—referred to as Third Isaiah because chapters 56–66 are written after the Jews returned to Jerusalem from Babylon and began the city's and the temple's restoration—that the LORD's house shall be called a house of prayer for all peoples, Jesus declares the temple to have become a den of thieves.

By driving out of the temple all economic activity, Jesus displays his authority to cleanse his Father's house, the same temple in which he was presented to God after his birth. Once cleansed, he can continue his teaching ministry, which is founded, of course, on prayer. Furthermore, Luke's Gospel opens with the scene of Zechariah offering incense in the temple while people are praying, and it closes with the apostles being "continually in the temple blessing God" (24:52). The new Israel (Gentiles) emerging from the old Israel (Jews) is Luke's theme. Thus, the old Israel's place of prayer (temple in Jerusalem) is the foundation for the new Israel's place of prayer in Rome, where the Acts of the Apostles ends.

Part 1

Before true prayer can begin one needs to cleanse his or her surroundings. The prayer corner, prayer room, or chapel needs to have removed anything that does not belong there, such as a TV, computer, phone, radio, etc. If the place of prayer is a church building, such things as dead plants, piles of papers, clutter of all kinds, bulletin boards layered with flyers vying for attention need to be cleaned. Taking the intention of the Lukan Jesus seriously would also eliminate selling chances on raffles, bingo as a source of revenue, and any other type of money-raising in the church.

Besides surroundings, one's heart also needs to be cleaned. Commonly referred to as conversion, heart-cleansing begins with a thorough examination of conscience. It continues with a purification of intention to pray, that is, to speak and to listen. Often, prayer becomes telling God what he needs to do instead of listening to God explain what he wants done. The heart must also be cleansed of the illusion of personal power, the anger of not getting one's way, self-righteousness, and more. As Jesus demonstrates, a temple, prayer corner, prayer room, chapel, or church needs to be cleansed before it truly becomes a house of prayer.

Meditation: What type of cleansing does your prayer place need? From what does your heart need to be cleaned before true prayer can occur in you?

Prayer: Almighty God, you declared your temple a house of prayer for all people, and your Son, Jesus Christ, cleansed it for that very reason. Cleanse my heart that it may be a house of prayer. Grant me the wisdom to recognize how all designated places of prayer can be enhanced by house cleaning. I ask this through my Lord, Jesus Christ, who lives and reigns with you and the Holy Spirit, one God, forever and ever. Amen.

Prayer in Luke's Gospel
ALERT PRAYER
(21:36): Saturday of the Thirty-Fourth Week in Ordinary Time, Years I & II

Scripture: Jesus said to his disciples, "Be alert at all times, praying that you may have the strength to escape all these things that will take place, and to stand before the Son of Man." (Luke 21:36)

Reflection: Jesus' concluding verse of his apocalyptic exhortation in Luke's Gospel is meant to echo the account of the prophet(ess) Anna, who, as a widow worshiped in the temple with fasting and prayer night and day. In other words, she kept vigil prayer. This is exactly the kind of prayer in which Jesus tells his disciples to engage; he calls it alert prayer.

At the time Luke's Gospel was written late in the first century, the expectation of the imminent coming of Jesus was waning. The author of this gospel both emphasizes that it is going to happen, but that it will not take place for a very long time. It is because it is not going to happen as soon as it was originally thought that Luke can write a volume about the activity of the apostles. No second volume would have been necessary if Jesus were returning very soon.

When Jesus returns, he will be looking for those who are alert, that is, those who are watchful in every season. Their alert prayer will give them strength to endure the events that are to come. That primary event is the destruction of Jerusalem and the temple by the Romans in 70 CE. The Lukan Jesus can predict Jerusalem's fall and the temple's demolishment because Luke is writing about the event twenty years after it happened. In fact, earlier in the apocalyptic discourse, he narrates some of the historical events that accompanied the event.

In Lukan understanding, the kingdom of God is here; it has been enacted by the words and deeds of Jesus. However, it is not yet here in its fullness. That's why Jesus tells his disciples that when they see "these things taking place," they should "know that the kingdom of God is near" (21:31). Likewise, their alert prayer

Part 1

should be for strength to stand before the Son of Man, that is, Jesus, when he returns in glory.

The best example of alert prayer is found in the Church's liturgy known as the Easter Vigil, often referred to as the mother of all vigils. This alert prayer takes place during the night. Beginning with a blazing fire from which a Paschal Candle is lit, worshipers remain alert by processing into the worship area. There, they listen to nine passages from the Bible, responding in song with psalms. Candidates for initiation are baptized and confirmed. The Eucharist is celebrated. And three to four hours later, the alert prayer is temporarily ended. A group of people have kept watch; they have not let "dissipation and drunkenness and the worries of this life" catch them "unexpectedly" (21:34).

Alert prayer also characterizes the last two to three weeks of the liturgical season of Ordinary Time and the first two weeks of Advent. The gospel passages present Jesus' words about alert prayer, namely, watching, keeping vigil. Passages from biblical letters further emphasize the same. Followers of Jesus in the first century and followers of Jesus in the twenty-first century need to be alert in prayer so that they are not caught surprised when Jesus returns.

Meditation: How often do you make alert prayer? How often do you pray for strength to escape the disasters that surround you? How often do you pray for the strength to stand before Christ in glory?

Prayer: Father of my Lord Jesus Christ, you promise that your Son will come again in glory. Fill me with the Holy Spirit that I may be kept alert in prayer. With the same Spirit strengthen me to withstand all calamities that come my way. And strengthen me to stand before the Son of Man when he comes. Hear this prayer through the same Christ, my Lord. Amen.

Prayer in Luke's Gospel

PRAYER FOR SIMON

(22:31–32): Palm Sunday of the Lord's Passion, Cycle C

Scripture: Jesus said, "Simon, Simon, listen! Satan has demanded to sift all of you like wheat, but I have prayed for you that your own faith may not fail; and you, when once you have turned back, strengthen your brothers." (Luke 22:31–32)

Reflection: After celebrating Passover with his disciples and mediating a dispute among them about who is the greatest, Jesus confers on them the Father's kingdom that he has been enacting through his words and deeds before telling Simon, otherwise known as Peter, that he has prayed that his faith may remain strong as he prepares for the last scenes of his life: the agony in the garden, his arrest, his crucifixion, and his death.

Satan is the adversary, who, as he does in the Book of Job, tests those leaders who have been appointed by Jesus, who himself was tested by Satan before beginning his ministry. It is important to note here that Satan is not the same as the devil or evil or demons. In the Book of Job, Satan is a member of God's court; he obtains permission from God to test Job, just like he obtains permission to test Jesus' apostles. Unique to Luke is a verse found earlier in the story, namely, "... Satan entered into Judas called Iscariot, who was one of the twelve" (22:3). In other words, Judas has been sifted and fell through the sieve.

Jesus has prayed that Peter's faith will not fail. He has petitioned God that he not let Simon's faith run out. As long as he keeps faith, he may fail, which indeed he does, but he can be rehabilitated—he can repent or be reconverted—and strengthen his fellow apostles. This prepares the reader for Peter's role as leader in the Acts of the Apostles.

As Jesus demonstrates, prayer for others—otherwise known as intercession—is a type of prayer of petition. Instead of praying for oneself, one petitions God for the good of others. When a person is asked by another to pray for him or her, the asker is requesting intercessory prayer. It may be for a good outcome for surgery or chemotherapy for cancer. It may be for safety on a journey. It may be for strength while grieving a relative's or friend's death. No matter what the need, that is, the occasion for sifting, the prayer, as Jesus demonstrates, is that the person's faith will not run out or fail.

Meditation: For whom have you recently interceded? What good did you ask God to grant him or her? In what ways did your prayer demonstrate that it was so that his or her faith did not fail during his or her time of testing?

Prayer: Ever-listening God, no prayer of intercession ever goes unheeded by you. Through whatever trials of daily life come my way, keep my faith strong. I ask this through my Lord, Jesus Christ, who himself prayed for Simon, and who lives and reigns with you and the Holy Spirit, who makes intercession for all according to your will, Father. You are one God, forever and ever. Amen.

EARNEST PRAYER

(22:40–45): Palm Sunday of the Lord's Passion, Cycle C

Scripture: "When [Jesus] reached the [Mount of Olives], he said to [the disciples], 'Pray that you may not come into the time of trial.' Then he withdrew from them about a stone's throw, knelt down, and prayed, 'Father, if you are willing, remove this cup from me; yet, not my will but yours be done.' Then an angel from heaven appeared to him and gave him strength. In his anguish he prayed more earnestly, and his sweat became like great drops of blood falling down on the ground. When he got up from prayer, he came to the disciples and found them sleeping because of grief . . . ." (Luke 22:40–45)

Reflection: Commonly referred to as the agony in the garden, this scene in Luke's Gospel is punctuated with themes that occur elsewhere in his narrative. The place of this scene—Mount of Olives—indicates how important it is in the gospel. A mountain is as close to God as one can get on the earth.

Prayer in Luke's Gospel

The Lukan Jesus instructs his disciples to pray that they may not have to undergo a time of trial. Jesus' words to the disciples echo that of a line in the prayer he taught them earlier in the narrative: "... [D]o not bring us to the time of trial" (11:4). Jesus wants his followers to pray that they are not tested, much like he told Simon that he prayed that he would not be tested earlier. While Jesus is praying, his disciples should be praying.

Jesus takes the posture of petitionary prayer: kneeling. His is a prayer of supplication, begging his Father to assist him to do his will. Jesus demonstrates that all prayer is about doing God's will. He petitions God to remove the cup, that is, his suffering, only if this fulfills his Father's will.

Jesus' prayer is answered. God sends an angel to strengthen him for the suffering that is about to begin. God wills that Jesus drink the cup. Once Jesus struggles with this reply, he enters into a deeper and more earnest prayer. With all the effort he can muster and like an athlete in a contest, he sweats, and his drops of sweat are like dribbles of blood plopping in the dust. But with the strength God has sent him, he is ready to enter into his passion.

Just like "they were weighed down with sleep" (9:32) during the transfiguration, so does Jesus find the disciples sleeping because of sorrow. Jesus had instructed them to pray while he prayed, but they fell asleep.

In times of physical trial, like hip surgery, chemotherapy treatment for cancer, or knee replacement, one should enter into earnest prayer. When dealing with stress at work, at home, at church, a person may discover strength through earnest prayer. Fervent prayer may assist when one is feeling unloved, unneeded, or unwanted.

During any time of agony, earnest prayer may result in a divine force of strength that enables the pray-er to muster all the effort he or she can in the struggle through the trial to do God's will.

Meditation: With what trial have you recently struggled? Did you pray to do God's will? Did you discover divine strength? Into what type of earnest prayer did you enter?

Part 1

Prayer: Mighty God, you strengthen those who earnestly desire to do your will. In my time of trial send the Holy Spirit as my strength and guide that I may imitate your Son, Jesus Christ, who lives and reigns with you, Father, and the Holy Spirit, one God, forever and ever. Amen.

FORGIVENESS PRAYER
(23:32–34): Palm Sunday of the Lord's Passion, Cycle C

Scripture: "Two others . . . , who were criminals, were led away to be put to death with [Jesus]. When they came to the place that is called The Skull, they crucified Jesus there with the criminals, one on his right and one on his left. Then Jesus said, 'Father, forgive them; for they do not know what they are doing.'" (Luke 23:32–34)

Reflection: The author of Luke's Gospel is very brief in his narrative description of Jesus' walk to The Skull. He says that two other criminals joined the execution party. He gives no description of the horrible form of execution named crucifixion. He gives no details of the death by asphyxiation caused by the crucified one's inability to push up his body in order to fill his lungs with air. The only detail that the reader is given is the first of two last prayers that Jesus says.

As he has done when in prayer throughout Luke's Gospel, Jesus addresses God as Father. Then, as he had taught his disciples to love their enemies and to pray for those who abuse them, he not only loves his enemies and prays for his abusers, but he asks God to forgive them for crucifying him, because his death is God's will and they are instruments of him doing his Father's will. They do not know that they are vehicles for God's will to be done; they do not know who Jesus is.

Forgiveness prayer is the antidote to hate, retaliation, and anger. Forgiveness prayer is all the tax collector can voice before God in the temple. Forgiveness prayer swings open the pray-er's self-locked prison door, setting free the one who may be tempted to choose one of the many ugly ways humans have found to nurse evil. Immediately after he is nailed to two pieces of wood, Jesus says a forgiveness prayer for those who have just put in motion the series of events that will shortly result in his death. By asking God to forgive those who crucified him, Jesus is also forgiving them.

Meditation: For whom do you need to offer a forgiveness prayer? What did he or she do to you in ignorance? Does asking God to forgive the person assist you in forgiving him or her? How?

Prayer: Father, your mercy is without measure to those who come to you seeking forgiveness. Hear my prayer for your forgiveness for any who have harmed or hurt me in any way. Grant me the grace to imitate your Son, who prayed for the forgiveness of those who crucified him. I ask this through the same Jesus Christ, who lives and reigns with you and the Holy Spirit, one God, forever and ever. Amen.

ABANDONMENT PRAYER

(23:46): Palm Sunday of the Lord's Passion, Cycle C

Scripture: ". . . Jesus, crying with a loud voice, said, 'Father, into your hands I commend my spirit.' Having said this, he breathed his last." (Luke 23:46)

Reflection: Throughout Luke's Gospel, Jesus is the Father's Son. In his last prayer in the narrative, he once again addresses God as Father and abandons himself into his Father's hands. The image is that of a human father standing at a distance from his child with open hands. The child runs toward his or her father, trusting that he will receive him or her and wrap his arms around the little one. In other words, the child trustingly abandons himself or herself into the hands of his or her father.

While the verse is from Psalm 31:5—"Into your hand I commit my spirit . . . , O LORD . . ."—it also serves as the act of Jesus returning the spirit he received when he was conceived by the Holy Spirit in the womb of his mother. By trustingly abandoning

Part 1

his spirit to the Father, he prepares for one of the opening scenes of the Acts of the Apostles: Pentecost, the outpouring of the Spirit upon everyone.

In Luke's Gospel, Jesus dies the death of a martyr; he is declared innocent by everyone. During his trial before Pilate, he is found innocent. One of the two crucified criminals declares him to be innocent. Even the centurion at the foot of the cross declares that he was an innocent man. So, it is appropriate that the innocent Jesus trustingly abandon his spirit into the hands of his Father.

Then, after saying his prayer, Jesus dies. His death becomes a model for his followers. Trustingly, they are to abandon their spirit to their Father, like a child abandons himself or herself into the hands of his or her father. Innocently, Jesus' followers are to give back to God what God has given to them, namely, their life and their spirit that was first breathed into them on the day of their conception.

Meditation: In what ways now do you trustingly abandon yourself into the Father's hands? How do these experiences prepare you to do the same at the hour of your death?

Prayer: Father, you are the source of all life, which you breathe into people at the moment of their conception. At the time of my death give me the courage to entrust my spirit into your hands. I ask this through my Lord, Jesus Christ, your Son, who lives and reigns with you and the Holy Spirit, one God, forever and ever. Amen.

PART 2

Prayer in the Acts of the Apostles

CONSTANT PRAYER

(1:13–14): Seventh Sunday of Easter, Cycle A; October 7

Scripture: ". . . Peter, and John, and James, and Andrew, Philip and Thomas, Bartholomew and Matthew, James son of Alphaeus, and Simon the Zealot, and Judas son of James . . . were constantly devoting themselves to prayer, together with certain women, including Mary the mother of Jesus, as well as his brothers." (Acts 1:13–14)

Reflection: Immediately following Jesus' ascension in the Acts of the Apostles, the narrator notes that the eleven apostles (Judas is omitted; the narrative explaining what happened to him follows the account of the apostles in prayer) returned to Jerusalem, according to Jesus' instruction before he left, and "went to the room upstairs where they were staying" (1:13) to await baptism with the Holy Spirit. While awaiting this gift, they focused on constant prayer.

Part 2

The mention of Mary the mother of Jesus is important at the beginning of the Acts of the Apostles. Since the author of Luke's Gospel and the author of the Acts is the same person, he presents Mary both at the beginning of the gospel and at the beginning of the Acts. In the gospel, Mary appears in the unique infancy narratives, but does not appear by name after that. She, who was overshadowed by the power of the Holy Spirit to conceive in her womb the Messiah, is present in the upstairs room-womb, in which the Holy Spirit will give birth to the church in a few days. Furthermore, in Luke's Gospel women have roles as disciples; likewise do they have roles as disciples in the Acts.

Their primary responsibility, like that of the apostles, is constant prayer. As its name may imply, constant prayer does not mean to be saying prayers all the time. Constant prayer is a mental attitude, a predisposition set in place in a person's life after practice. Instead of cooking a meal because food is needed, a person with a perspective of constant prayer makes the cooking of the meal a prayer, entering intentionally into the process of preparing food, keeping in mind those who will be nourished by it, and doing this for God's glory.

Instead of playing a sport only to win, one who has practiced constant prayer enters into the game with the intention of making every play a prayer of praise to his or her Creator. The player gets lost in the sport; that is, he or she gets lost in prayer at play. In so doing, the person plays for the glory of God. Likewise, work can be labor or it can be a form of constant prayer. Instead of seeing work as labor, the pray-er does his or her work for God's glory.

Prayer is a way of life. To maintain constant prayer reminders are needed, such as time taken for morning and evening prayer, grace before and after meals, etc. Sunday is kept holy through prayer. The liturgical year with its cycle of seasons and feasts further enhances the constant prayer of Christians.

Meditation: What are the marks of constant prayer in your life? How is your life one of constant prayer? What further steps do you need to take to make more of your life a constant prayer?

Prayer in the Acts of the Apostles

Prayer: Eternal Father, you fill your people with your Holy Spirit that they may be always in your presence. Grant me the grace of constant prayer so that whatever I do in thought, word, and deed may give you glory. I ask this through Jesus Christ, my Lord, who lives and reigns with you and the Holy Spirit, one God, forever and ever. Amen.

REPLACEMENT PRAYER
(1:23–26): Seventh Sunday of Easter, Cycle B; May 14

Scripture: The believers ". . . proposed two [candidates to replace Judas], Joseph called Barsabbas, who was also known as Justus, and Matthias. Then they prayed and said, 'Lord, you know everyone's heart. Show us which one of these two you have chosen to take the place in this ministry and apostleship from which Judas turned aside to go to his own place.' And they cast lots for them, and the lot fell on Matthias; and he was added to the eleven apostles." (Acts 1:23–26)

Reflection: Before the election of a new apostle to replace Judas, Peter gives a short speech explaining what happened to Judas—namely, he fell headlong into a field, burst open, and all his bowels gushed out. Then, Peter, functioning as the leader he demonstrated himself to be in Luke's Gospel when he correctly answered Jesus' question about Jesus' identity, proposes that another apostle needs to be chosen to replace Judas so that the twelve are reconstituted before Pentecost.

Two potential apostles are nominated: Justus and Matthias. After the two are nominated, all pray. The author of the Acts records the prayer they said. It begins with the statement that God knows everyone's heart. This is a theme that permeates the Bible. Since God is the creator who is all-knowing, it only follows that he knows everyone's intentions. Then, all present ask God to reveal which of the men God has chosen. In other words, they make a replacement prayer. Just like Jesus prayed before choosing twelve

Part 2

apostles from his disciples in Luke's Gospel, so the apostles pray before reconstituting the twelve in the Acts of the Apostles.

Then, in order to know which man God has chosen to be apostle number twelve, they cast lots. Usually compared to rolling dice, casting lots is a form of divination, that is, a way to determine God's will. One name or initial was inscribed on a stone and another name or initial was inscribed on another stone. Both stones were placed in a clay jar and shaken until one came out. The one that emerged first indicated which man God had chosen for the ministry of apostleship.

Matthias is determined to be God's choice. He is added to the eleven to bring the number back to twelve. The number of apostles must be restored because in the view of the author of Acts the new Israel (Christianity) emerges out of the old Israel (Judaism). Just as the old Israel was founded on the twelve sons of Jacob, so the new Israel is founded on the twelve apostles.

Replacement prayer is very important in the life of a Christian. Often, a new president of a committee or group needs to be replaced. Instead of deciding who will be president based on democracy, why not try replacement prayer? After two or three are nominated, stop and ask God whom he chooses for the office. Then, cast ballots. Instead of determining the will of the people, why not determine the will of God through replacement prayer?

Meditation: To what groups do you belong where replacement prayer would be most appropriate? How might you introduce it?

Prayer: Lord God, you know the thoughts of every person you created. Help me to discern your will in my life; then, send your Holy Spirit to help me carry out that will. I ask this in the name of Jesus Christ, your Son, who lives and reigns with you and the Holy Spirit, one God, forever and ever, Amen.

Prayer in the Acts of the Apostles

THE PRAYERS

(2:41–42): Second Sunday of Easter, Cycle A

Scripture: ". . . [T]hose who welcomed [Peter's] message were baptized, and that day about three thousand persons were added. They devoted themselves to the apostles' teaching and fellowship, to the breaking of bread and the prayers." (Acts 2:41–42)

Reflection: After the event of Pentecost, Peter delivers a sermon to the Jews in which he explains how Hebrew Bible (Old Testament) texts have been fulfilled. Peter concludes his remarks by stating, ". . . [L]et the entire house of Israel know with certainty that God has made him both Lord and Messiah, this Jesus whom you crucified" (2:36). Those listening to Peter ask him what they need to do, and he informs them that they need to repent and be baptized and they will receive the Holy Spirit. About three thousand do.

This community of the baptized is characterized by four elements. First, the members devote themselves to the apostles' teaching. The apostles continue the teaching ministry of Jesus which was begun in Luke's Gospel. Second, the members devote themselves to fellowship; this is later explained as being together and holding all things in common, selling possessions and goods and distributing the proceeds to all, as any have need.

Third, the baptized are devoted to the breaking of bread, one of the earliest titles used for the celebration of Eucharist or Mass. Eating meals together is a very strong theme throughout Luke's Gospel, so it is no surprise that it appears here. The risen Christ is recognized in the breaking of bread. Fourth, the members of the community of the baptized devote themselves to the prayers. This means they live a life of prayer.

These four elements are not parts that form a whole; they are united as spirituality, a way of life lived under the influence of the Holy Spirit. Luke's idealized portrait does not separate worship and service; the author understands them to flow in and out of each other. Baptized believers form a society which relies upon apostolic teaching, unity, the common meal, and devotion or prayer.

Part 2

All of these characteristics express worship; all of these characteristics express service. In other words, the narrator presents a very integrated and functioning community.

This understanding gleaned from the Acts of the Apostles serves as an antidote in a culture that separates everything. For most people worship is going to church and hearing a homily or a sermon, which may or may not further push apart worship and service. Service is understood to be helping others through volunteer work and contributing to agencies that help the homeless and poor. Eucharist is a once-a-week activity for the purpose of receiving communion. And if there are any daily prayers, that time is isolated from the rest of the day.

The ideal that the author of the Acts presents is that of an integrated life of worship and service under the direction of the Holy Spirit. The integration of apostolic instruction within the community of believers leads to Eucharist and prayers, and Eucharist and prayers lead to more apostolic instruction within the community. Spirituality, the influence of the Holy Spirit, fosters the wholeness of individuals and the community or the wholeness of the community and the individuals who form it.

Meditation: What is your personal experience of the integration of worship and service? What is your experience of the integration of worship and service as a member of a community?

Prayer: God of holiness, through your Son you have taught your people to be whole. Guide me with the Holy Spirit that I may understand how spirituality flows out of the integration of worship and service. Grant me the grace to live my life devoted to the teaching of the apostles and their successors, to community, to the breaking of bread, and to the prayers. I ask this through my Lord Jesus Christ, who lives and reigns with you and the Holy Spirit, one God, forever and ever. Amen.

Prayer in the Acts of the Apostles

HOUR OF PRAYER

(3:1–2): Wednesday of the Octave of Easter, Years I & II; June 29 (Vigil)

Scripture: "One day Peter and John were going up to the temple at the hour of prayer, at three o'clock in the afternoon. And a man lame from birth was being carried in. People would lay him daily at the gate of the temple called the Beautiful Gate so that he could ask for alms from those entering the temple." (Acts 3:1–2)

Reflection: The author of the Acts of the Apostles is the same person who wrote Luke's Gospel. In the gospel, the temple plays an important role because the author understands that the new Israel (Christianity) is birthed by the old Israel (Judaism). The temple is not only the locus for many of the events of Jesus' life, but it is also the setting for many events in the apostles' lives.

Such is the case when Peter and John were preparing to observe the three o'clock hour of prayer, the traditional Jewish time of the evening sacrifice. The books of Exodus and Numbers describe the evening sacrifice as a burnt offering of a lamb with flour and oil. While the two apostles are approaching the temple, a lame man, being carried by others, is also simultaneously approaching it.

The lame man asks Peter and John for alms—a traditional Jewish obligation—which they do not have to give. However, what they do have is stated by Peter: ". . . [W]hat I have I give you; in the name of Jesus Christ of Nazareth, stand up and walk" (3:6). And with those alms, the man is healed. Thus, like Jesus healed a cripple in Luke's Gospel, Peter and John heal a lame man; and later in the Acts, Paul heals a man crippled from birth. The action of the apostles' healing paralleling Jesus' healing is a theme woven through Luke and Acts.

What is more important to notice is the time of the healing; it is the hour of prayer, the time of sacrifice. The apostles offer the name of Jesus Christ of Nazareth to the lame man at the same time as the lamb is being offered in the temple. While the theme of Jesus

Part 2

being the Lamb of God is more pronounced in John's Gospel, it is present here, too. The One who died on the cross as a sacrifice to bring healing to the whole world continues to heal through his followers. The time of this healing corresponds with the hour of prayer.

The simplest of prayers is that of repetition of the name "Jesus." The *Catechism of the Catholic Church* says, "The invocation of the holy name of Jesus is the simplest way of praying always."[1] Furthermore, it teaches:

> The name "Jesus" contains all: God and man [and woman] and the whole economy of creation and salvation. To pray "Jesus" is to invoke him and to call him within us. His name is the only one that contains the presence it signifies. Jesus is the Risen One, and whoever invokes the name of Jesus is welcoming the Son of God who loved him and who gave himself up for him.[2]

Spending an hour repeating the name of Jesus is possible anywhere and at anytime.

Meditation: Spend an hour repeating the name of the Jesus. How did the prayer make your heart more attentive? How did the hour of prayer deepen your love for God?

Prayer: Lord Jesus Christ, you are the Son of God, the Word of God, the Lamb of God. As I repeat your name in prayer, open my heart to the stirring of the Holy Spirit and draw me more deeply into the love you share with your Father and the Holy Spirit, with whom you live and reign as one God, forever and ever. Amen.

---

1. *Catechism*, par. 268.
2. Ibid., par. 2666.

Prayer in the Acts of the Apostles
PRAYER FOR BOLDNESS
(4:24–25a, 26–31): Monday of the Second Week of Easter, Years I & II

Scripture: Peter and John prayed: "'Sovereign Lord, who made the heaven and the earth, the sea, and everything in them, it is you who [spoke] by the Holy Spirit through our ancestor David, your servant. For in this city, in fact, both Herod and Pontius Pilate, with the Gentiles and the people of Israel, gathered together against your holy servant Jesus, whom you anointed, to do whatever your hand and your plan had predestined to take place. And now, Lord, look at their threats, and grant to your servants to speak your word with all boldness, while you stretch out your hand to heal, and signs and wonders are performed through the name of your holy servant Jesus.' When they had prayed, the place in which they were gathered together was shaken; and they were all filled with the Holy Spirit and spoke the word of God with boldness." (Acts 4:24–25a, 26–31)

Reflection: After healing a lame man, Peter delivers a speech calling the Jews to repentance for the forgiveness of their sins. Peter and John are arrested by the temple guard and imprisoned. The next day they are brought before the Jewish authorities and Peter, filled with the Holy Spirit, delivers another speech proclaiming "the name of Jesus Christ of Nazareth" (4:10). After conferring among themselves, the authorities order Peter and John "not to speak or teach at all in the name of Jesus" (4:18). Peter and John inform the authorities that they cannot obey their order. Once released, Peter and John go to their friends and pray.

Their prayer begins with the acknowledgment of God as Creator of everything. Not only did God create all that exists, but he also spoke by the Holy Spirit through King David's Psalm 2. Peter and John understand that the words of Psalm 2—about the rage of the Gentiles—have been fulfilled in the actions of Herod, Pilate, the Gentiles, and the Jews in crucifying God's Anointed. The

Part 2

prayer concludes with the apostles' request that God protect them from the threats of the Jewish authorities and grant them boldness to speak his word while he performs signs and wonders when the name of Jesus is spoken. As soon as they finish praying, the presence of God is signified by the house shaking and their being filled with the Holy Spirit, who enables them to speak with boldness. In other words, their prayer is granted.

The prayer of boldness is needed when faced with anything which threatens the silencing of God's truth. For example, a pastor may be faced with a threat of leaving the parish by a small group of parishioners who desire something that is not good for the whole parish; he needs to pray for boldness. Likewise, when teaching people about the moral positions of the Catholic Church, instructors should pray for boldness before presenting their material to a culture that thinks it can do whatever it feels like doing. Even among friends, a prayer of boldness is needed before telling the other person that something he or she did is wrong. The house will probably not shake, but God promises to fill with the Holy Spirit those who call upon the name of Jesus so that their words are spoken with boldness.

Meditation: When have you recently prayed a prayer for boldness? What was the threat? How did you speak the name of Jesus? What sign let you know that God filled you with the Holy Spirit of boldness?

Prayer: Sovereign Lord, maker of heaven and earth, the sea, and everything in them, in the past you have spoken by the Holy Spirit through prophets, priests, and kings. In the fullness of time, you spoke by the Holy Spirit through the incarnation of your Son. Give me boldness to speak your word, so that you may perform signs and wonders in the name of Jesus Christ, who lives and reigns with you and the Holy Spirit, one God, forever and ever. Amen.

Prayer in the Acts of the Apostles

SERVING PRAYER

(6:2–4): Fifth Sunday of Easter, Cycle A; Saturday of the Second Week of Easter, Years I & II

Scripture: "... [T]he twelve called together the whole community of the disciples and said, 'It is not right that we should neglect the word of God in order to wait on tables. Therefore, friends, select from among yourselves seven men of good standing, full of the Spirit and of wisdom, whom we may appoint to this task, while we, for our part, will devote ourselves to prayer and to serving the word.'" (Acts 6:2–4)

Reflection: The narrator of the Acts of the Apostles tells the reader that the number of followers of Jesus is increasing. However, Greek-speaking disciples are complaining against Hebrew (Aramaic)-speaking followers because their widows are being neglected in the daily distribution of food. Just like Jesus had appointed twelve and seventy (or seventy-two) as leaders, so the twelve decide to appoint seven who would be responsible for serving this need of the community.

As the text indicates, the twelve have a responsibility to pray and serve the word of God, that is, like the twelve sons of Jacob (the old Israel), the twelve apostles (the new Israel) are responsible for furthering God's mission. When others can be appointed to a task, such as overseeing the soup kitchen, they should be given the responsibility. This later becomes known as the principle of subsidiarity, namely,

> a community of a higher order should not interfere in the internal life of a community of a lower order, depriving the latter of its functions, but rather should support it in case of need and help to co-ordinate its activity with the activities of the rest of society, always with a view to the common good.[3]

After the community chooses seven men to wait on tables, it "had these men stand before the apostles, who prayed and laid

---

3. Ibid., 1883.

Part 2

their hands on them" (6:6). In other words, the apostles remain true to their mission of devoting themselves to prayer and serving the word of God. Just as Jesus laid hands upon others to heal, the apostles lay hands to heal, to bestow the Holy Spirit, and to commission for ministry, as in this scene.

It is out of prayer that the word of God is served. In other words, the mission is furthered only out of prayer, because prayer is the means to access God's will for the next step of the mission, as here in delegating seven men to oversee the part of the mission that involves taking care of the needs of widows. Thus, to serve prayer is to serve the word of God.

Most people may not think about serving prayer, but the metaphor is apt in the Acts of the Apostles. To serve prayer is to lead a life characterized by prayer from which flows the furthering of God's kingdom. Traditionally, prayer can be served before meals. Prayer can be served before leaving home. Prayer can be served upon rising in the morning and before retiring at night. Through prayer, the pray-er is connected to God by the Holy Spirit, who relays the next step to take in God's mission. The author of the Acts of the Apostles understands that prayer is a prerequisite to any mission activity. Furthermore, according to the Acts, God often instructs that others be appointed to responsibility for a part of the mission.

Meditation: When have you most recently served prayer? What mission did that prayer reveal? Were you instructed to appoint any others to take responsibility for a part of the mission?

Prayer: Mighty God, you continue to spread your word through those who remain in prayer with you. Grant that I may be devoted to prayer and to serving your word. Fill me with the Holy Spirit of guidance that I might serve you faithfully. Hear me in the name of Jesus Christ, your Son, who lives and reigns with you and the Holy Spirit, one God, forever and ever. Amen.

Prayer in the Acts of the Apostles

STEPHEN'S PRAYER

(6:8–10, 12; 7:51, 54, 58–60): Monday and Tuesday of the Third Week of Easter, Years I & II; December 26

Scripture: "Stephen, full of grace and power, did great wonders and signs among the people. Then some of those who belong to the synagogue of the Freedmen . . . stood up and argued with Stephen. But they could not withstand the wisdom and the Spirit with which he spoke. They stirred up the people as well as the elders and the scribes; then they suddenly confronted him, seized him, and brought him before the council. [Stephen said,] 'You stiff-necked people, uncircumcised in heart and ears, you are forever opposing the Holy Spirit, just as your ancestors used to do.' When they heard these things, they became enraged and ground their teeth at Stephen. Then they dragged him out of the city and began to stone him . . . . While they were stoning Stephen, he prayed, 'Lord Jesus, receive my spirit.' Then he knelt down and cried out in a loud voice, 'Lord, do not hold this sin against them.' When he had said this, he died." (Acts 6:8–10, 12; 7:51, 54, 58–60)

Reflection: The narrative concerning Stephen, one of the seven men chosen by the apostles to wait on tables, occupies half of chapter six and the entire lengthy chapter seven in the Acts of the Apostles. Stephen, a man described as "a man full of faith and the Holy Spirit" (6:5), follows in the footsteps of the apostles by serving the word of God.

Stephen, whose name means "crown," is an almost exact copy of Jesus. Stephen's words are informed by the Holy Spirit, just like Jesus' teaching was done after prayer in the Holy Spirit. Like Jesus gives three speeches or discourses in Luke's Gospel, so Stephen gives one, long summary of the Hebrew Bible (Old Testament), focusing on the stiff-necked people, who, like their ancestors, oppose the Holy Spirit, who spoke through the prophets and now through Stephen.

Part 2

Just like Jesus was interrogated by the Jewish leaders, so is Stephen interrogated by them. Just as Jesus was found guilty, so is Stephen found guilty. Just as Jesus is crucified, Stephen is stoned. Just as Jesus entrusts his spirit to God, so Stephen asks Jesus to receive his spirit. And just as Jesus asks God to forgive those who crucify him, Stephen asks God not to hold his death against them. Thus, in Stephen is traced Jesus. While Jesus received a crown of thorns, Stephen is crowned with martyrdom; in other words, he bears witness to his faith all the way to his death, even though, like Jesus, he is innocent of all crimes.

Stephen's prayer is one of submission, as indicated by his kneeling down, much like Simon Peter falls down before Jesus after catching a net full of fish, a unique story in Luke's Gospel that becomes a post-resurrection narrative in John's Gospel. Submission is not a popular word, because it carries negative connotations in a culture that refuses to bend its knee to any authority. In reference to God and Jesus, however, the author of Luke-Acts understands the act of yielding to the will of God in positive terms; that is, submission, like that of Jesus and Stephen to God's will, brings with it a profound freedom. And this, of course, is the paradox: One is only free to preach God's word if one has first submitted to God's will through prayer.

Meditation: When have you submitted yourself to God's will through prayer? How do you experience your culture pulling you in the opposite direction? What freedom did you experience through your act of submission to God?

Prayer: Father, I kneel before you, creator of heaven and earth. Inspire my spirit with your Holy Spirit that I may know your will and do it. Do not hold the sin of my persecutors against them, but grant them forgiveness in the name of Jesus, your Son, who lives and reigns with you and the Holy Spirit, one God forever and ever. Amen.

Prayer in the Acts of the Apostles

PRAYER FOR THE HOLY SPIRIT

(8:14–16): Sixth Sunday of Easter, Cycle A

Scripture: ". . . [W]hen the apostles at Jerusalem heard that Samaria had accepted the word of God, they sent Peter and John to them. The two went down and prayed for them that they might receive the Holy Spirit (for as yet the Spirit had not come upon any of them; they had only been baptized in the name of the Lord Jesus)." (Acts 8:14–16)

Reflection: After the death of Stephen, another one of the seven men appointed to wait on tables—Philip—goes to Samaria and proclaims Jesus as the Messiah to the people there and works signs and wonders. It is important for the reader to note that this move from Jerusalem to Samaria is the reverse of Jesus' move from Samaria to Jerusalem. The author of Luke-Acts uses geography as a means to organize both books. In the gospel, Jesus journeys from Galilee through Samaria to Judea and Jerusalem; in the Acts, the apostles journey from Jerusalem through Judea to Samaria and, finally, to the end of the earth: Rome.

In Samaria, many "believed Philip, who was proclaiming the good news about the kingdom of God and the name of Jesus Christ" and "they were baptized, both men and women" (8:12). Like Jesus' mission of proclaiming the kingdom of God, Philip participates in it by doing the same. However, because the author is interested in having this new part of the mission confirmed by the apostles, he is careful to note that believers did not receive the Holy Spirit when they were baptized. So, Peter and John are sent to Samaria. There, they pray that the believers will receive the Holy Spirit. Then, they lay their hands on them, and they receive the Holy Spirit.

The *Catechism of the Catholic Church* teaches, "Every time we begin to pray to Jesus it is the Holy Spirit who draws us on the way of prayer by his prevenient grace."[4] In other words, God, by the Holy Spirit, fills believers with grace before they pray, even before

---

4. Ibid., par. 2670.

they think of prayer. The Holy Spirit prepares believers for prayer. The *Catechism* says, "... [T]he Church invites [people] to call upon the Holy Spirit every day, especially at the beginning and the end of every important action."[5]

While "the traditional form of petition to the Holy Spirit is to invoke the Father through Christ our Lord to give us the Consoler Spirit,"[6] the simplest and most direct prayer to the Holy Spirit is this: "Come, Holy Spirit." This is the simple prayer of Peter and John. Again, the *Catechism* teaches, "The Holy Spirit, whose anointing permeates our whole being, is the interior master of Christian prayer."[7] There are as many ways to pray as there are pray-ers, "but it is the same Spirit acting in all and with all," states the *Catechism*. "It is in the communion of the Holy Spirit that Christian prayer is prayer in the Church."[8]

Meditation: How do you pray for the Holy Spirit? What signs indicate that you have received the Holy Spirit?

Prayer: Come, Holy Spirit, fill my heart and enkindle in me the fire of your love. As you once anointed believers with your power through the hands of Peter and John, now guide me in furthering the kingdom of God. Hear me through my Lord Jesus Christ, who lives and reigns with you and the Father, one God, forever and ever. Amen.

PRAYER GIFT

(8:18–20, 22)

Scripture: "... [W]hen Simon [, the magician,] saw that the Spirit was given through the laying on of the apostles' hands, he offered them money, saying, 'Give me also this power so that anyone on whom I lay my hands may receive the Holy Spirit.' But Peter said

5. Ibid.,
6. Ibid., par. 2671.
7. Ibid., par. 2672.
8. Ibid., par. 2673.

Prayer in the Acts of the Apostles

to him, 'May your silver perish with you, because you thought you could obtains God's gift with money! Repent therefore of this wickedness of yours, and pray to the Lord that, if possible, the intent of your heart may be forgiven you.'" (Acts 8:18–20, 22)

Reflection: In Samaria, Philip, one of the seven men chosen to wait on tables, encounters "a certain man named Simon [who] had previously practiced magic in the city and amazed the people of Samaria" (8:9). Despite this, Simon believes and is baptized by Philip. After Peter and John pray and lay their hands on the believers in Samaria, they receive the Holy Spirit. When Simon, the magician, sees this, he attempts to buy the power of giving the Holy Spirit from the apostles.

Peter immediately curses him for attempting to obtain God's gift with money. Then, Peter calls Simon to repent of his deed and to pray for forgiveness. The apostles do not control the Holy Spirit by laying their hands on the heads of believers; they are instruments, vehicles, of God's gift. Simon, even though baptized, has not yet been fully converted; in other words, he is still looking for ways to practice magic. There is no magic in the divine gift; it is freely given through those appointed by Jesus.

Simon the magician represents the easy way out and the more glorious way. He had already amazed the citizens of Samaria with his magic, so that they thought he possessed the power of God; they called him great. Philip, however, had won over the people of Samaria with his preaching about Jesus the Messiah. Simon feigns belief in order to have access to this power that Philip has.

What Simon learns is that the sign is not the gift; the sign of the laying on of hands points to God's gift. Peter and John do not manipulate God into giving his gift; they are but instruments that mediate it. Simon wants to posses the power to give the Spirit by making it contingent upon his act of laying his hands on others. Because of his desire to buy this spiritual position, later generations named any such act simony. The gift of the Holy Spirit is not about skill; it is about faith and openness to receive God's gift. Simon may finally understand this when he says to Peter, "Pray for me to the Lord, that nothing of what you have said may happen to me" (8:24).

The cultural position that people have to work hard to earn everything they have often gets in the way of openness to receive God's freely-given gift. As this story teaches, the Holy Spirit cannot be bought. It is a gift; God gives one of the tree persons of the Trinity to people, who are open to receive it. That gift—called grace—is even given to people beforehand in order to prepare them to be able to respond to the offer of the Holy Spirit. In other words, much like Philip prepared the people of Samaria for Peter and John, God prepares people for the Holy Spirit. A prayer gift is nothing other than remembering God, the source of everything.

Meditation: When have you most often received the gift of prayer? How did the Holy Spirit spark your prayer and bring you into deeper prayer? What often gets in the way of accepting this prayer gift from God?

Prayer: Lord God, giver of every gift, rain your grace upon your servant to prepare me to receive the gift of yourself, the Holy Spirit. With open hands and open heart I earnestly desire to receive him who unites me to you. You live and reign as one God—Father, Son, and Holy Spirit—forever and ever. Amen.

SAUL AT PRAYER

(9:10–12): Friday of the Third Week of Easter, Years I & II;
January 25 (Second Option)

Scripture: "Now there was a disciple in Damascus named Ananias. The Lord said to him in a vision, 'Ananias.' He answered, 'Here I am, Lord.' The Lord said to him, 'Get up and go to the street called Straight, and at the house of Judas look for a man of Tarsus named Saul. At this moment he is praying, and he has seen in a vision a man named Ananias come in and lay his hands on him so that he might regain his sight.'" (Acts 9:10–12)

Prayer in the Acts of the Apostles

Reflection: Saul, to whom the reader is first introduced at the stoning of Stephen, continues his mission of destroying Jewish Christianity until he is confronted by Jesus as he approaches Damascus and is blinded by a light from heaven. After discovering that he has been persecuting Jesus, Saul enters Damascus and fasts for three days. Meanwhile, in Damascus there is a disciple named Ananias, whom God sends to heal Saul while he is in prayer.

Fasting and prayer go together. Fasting prepares the pray-er for prayer, and prayer leads the fast-er back to fasting. Even though Saul is a persecutor of the Church, through fasting and prayer he prepares himself for a further revelation from God or a deeper understanding of the vision he already received. This is an important turning point in the Acts, as this account will be narrated two more times before the author finishes the book.

God is very specific in his directions to Ananias, who is given the name of the street, the owner of the house, and the name and place of origin of the blind man fasting and praying there. This would be equivalent to having the name of the resident of the house, the house number and street name, the city, state, and zip code. There is no doubt that Saul's vision and Ananias' vision are part of God's plan.

After an objection, Ananias fulfills God's plan. He goes to the house, enters it, and lays his hands on Saul, saying to him, "Brother Saul, the Lord Jesus, who appeared to you on your way here, has sent me so that you may regain your sight and be filled with the Holy Spirit" (9:17). The narrator resumes the story, telling the reader that something like scales fell from Saul's eyes and his sight was restored. Then, he was baptized, ate some food, and regained his strength. Thus, Saul, the man determined to stop Jewish Christianity, is converted to the very movement he sought to destroy. He begins to proclaim that Jesus is the Son of God.

It is humanly amazing what God can do in the lives of those who pry open themselves through fasting and prayer. Spiritual fasting is not greatly respected today, maybe because it has become associated with dieting in an over-weight culture. While spiritual fasting is more than just abstaining from food to lose weight, there remains the element of physically emptying oneself so that the person can be filled with prayer. If a person is already full—both physically and spiritually—there is nothing to fill. Emptiness through fasting and prayer prepares one for the work of God in his or her life.

Meditation: When have you entered into a prolonged period of fasting and prayer? With what did God fill your emptiness? What work or mission did you receive?

Prayer: Here I am, Lord. I come into your presence seeking to do your will. Strengthen me through fasting and prayer to receive your revelation. Strengthen me with the Holy Spirit to know your will and to do it. I ask this through Jesus Christ, my Lord, who lives and reigns with you and the Holy Spirit, one God, forever and ever. Amen.

PETER'S PRAYER

(9:36–37a, 40): Saturday of the Third Week of Easter, Years I & II

Scripture: "... [I]n Joppa there was a disciple whose name was Tabitha, which in Greek is Dorcas. She was devoted to good works and acts of charity. At that time she became ill and died. Peter put all of [the weeping widows] outside [the upstairs room], and then he knelt down and prayed. He turned to the body and said, 'Tabitha, get up.' Then she opened her eyes, and seeing Peter, she sat up." (Acts 9:36–37a, 40)

Reflection: Peter is the leader of the Jewish-Christian movement in the first part of the Acts of the Apostles. He travels around Palestine, visiting believers and healing them. Before he goes to Joppa, he is found in Lydda, where he heals a bedridden man named Aeneas. Just like Jesus heals a paralyzed man in Luke's Gospel, Peter heals a man paralyzed for eight years.

This first of two heroes of the Acts of the Apostles (the other is Paul), then travels to Joppa, where Peter again imitates Jesus.

This time, he raises a dead woman, like Jesus raised a little girl in the gospel. The result of Peter's healing and raising the dead is that many believe in the Lord. The work that occurs through Peter is the same work as Jesus did. In other words, the risen One continues his ministry through the life of Peter and the other apostles.

Peter's act of kneeling down and praying before he commands Tabitha to get up demonstrates this. In kneeling, he submits himself to Christ, much like he submitted himself to Jesus in the gospel. He becomes the means or the vehicle for the healing ministry of Jesus to continue. The author wants the reader to understand that the conversion of believers is not merely for the purpose of restoring them to health. Every new believer presents the risen Christ with the opportunity to continue his work through the Holy Spirit. In other words, through their prayer, believers become better instrument of Jesus; they are conformed more and more to him through prayer.

Meditation: In what ways have you been an instrument of the risen Christ bringing healing and new life to others? What role did the prayer of submission serve in your instrumentality? How, like Peter, were you conformed more to Jesus?

Prayer: Lord God, your Son continued his ministry of healing through the ministry of his apostles, especially that of Peter, and gradually conformed them to his image. Through the Holy Spirit, open me in prayer that I may be a worthy instrument of your work and be more and more shaped into the ministry of Jesus Christ, who lives and reigns with you and the Holy Spirit, one God, forever and ever. Amen.

PRAYERFUL CORNELIUS

(10:1–4)

Scripture: "In Caesarea there was a man named Cornelius, a centurion of the Italian Cohort, as it was called. He was a devout man who feared God with his entire household; he gave alms generously to the people and prayed constantly to God. One afternoon at about three o'clock he had a vision in which he clearly saw an angle of God coming in and saying to him, 'Cornelius.' He stared at him in terror and said, 'What is it, Lord?' He answered, 'Your prayers and your alms have ascended as a memorial before God.'" (Acts 10:1–4)

Reflection: Thus begins the three-chapter turning point in the Acts of the Apostles. While the material on prayer is focused on here, it is important for the reader to understand how this part of the story works as the turning point in the Acts.

Cornelius, a Gentile, is described by the narrator as a righteous man; he is devout, he fears God, he gives alms, and he prays. Thus, while he is not a convert to Judaism, he follows Torah and lives according to it. In this specific case, his whole household—family and servants—follows his lead. Also, the account of this centurion is meant to echo the narrative about Jesus and the centurion in Luke's Gospel.

Cornelius' vision occurs at the traditional hour of prayer. Like the double vision of Saul and Ananias earlier in the Acts, the narrator will explain that Peter has a vision around noon the next day. Cornelius is told by the angel in his vision to send for Peter; as in Ananias' vision, the angel gives specific directions as to where he can be found. While Peter is praying, he has a vision, which will be explored in the next section. In short, Peter, a Jewish Christian, will be instructed to launch the mission to the Gentiles. A Gentile Pentecost will occur, and after this, narratives about Saul's three missionary trips to the Gentiles will bring the Acts of the Apostles to a close.

The focus here is on the constant prayer of the Gentile Cornelius, a leader of about one hundred men within a cohort of about six hundred men. He is devout, meaning he is specifically religious or reverent toward the LORD, usually phrased as fearing God. Others like Cornelius prove to be fertile ground for the Christian mission, especially after the meeting in Jerusalem where the apostles decide that circumcision is not necessary.

Prayer in the Acts of the Apostles

The narrator tells the reader that Cornelius gives alms generously. Giving alms is an honored Jewish tradition at which this centurion excels. Furthermore, he prays constantly, a characteristic of the Jewish-Christian community. In other words, Cornelius and his household, that is, his community, are as close to being Jewish Christians as they can, even though they are Gentiles.

Being prayerful, literally being full of prayer, sets the stage for Cornelius' vision. Being devoted to and fearing God and giving alms prepare a person for prayer. Consistently through Luke's Gospel and the Acts of the Apostles, it is while characters are prayerful that they receive visions or messages from God.

While at first glance many people may think that visions are phenomena of the past, they continue in the lives of the prayerful today. The vision may be an insight that comes from reading the Bible. It may be a word spoken by another that seems to awaken the hearer from a deep sleep. A vision may come through a mentor or spiritual director indicating a course for the counseled to take. While being prayerful, Cornelius experienced a vision; the same happens today.

Meditation: When have you most recently had a vision while being prayerful? What did you interpret the vision to mean? How did you respond to the vision?

Prayer: Ever-living God, you never cease to reveal your will to those who are devout and fear you. With the Holy Spirit move my heart to generosity and open it to prayer that I may stand before you ready to receive a vision of your will for me. Hear this prayer through Jesus Christ, your Son, who lives and reigns with you and the Holy Spirit, one God, forever and ever. Amen.

PETER'S VISIONARY PRAYER

(10:9–11, 16–17a, 19–20)

Scripture: "About noon the next day [after Cornelius had a vision], as [Cornelius' two slaves] were on their journey [to Joppa]

Part 2

and approaching the city, Peter went up on the roof to pray. He became hungry and wanted something to eat; and while it was being prepared, he fell into a trance. He saw the heaven opened and something like a large sheet coming down, being lowered to the ground by its four corners. This happened three times, and the thing was suddenly taken up to heaven. Now, while Peter was greatly puzzled about what to make of the vision that he had seen, suddenly the men sent by Cornelius appeared. While Peter was still thinking about the vision, the Spirit said to him, 'Look, three men are searching for you. Now get up, go down and go with them without hesitation; for I have sent them.'" (Acts 10:9–11, 16–17a, 19–20)

Reflection: Like Cornelius previously, Peter has a vision while he is being prayerful and becomes hungry. Like at Jesus' baptism and transfiguration the heaven opens, so does the heaven open while Peter is in a trance. Divine revelation is being given to Peter in the form of a large sheet filled with "all kinds of four-footed creatures and reptiles and birds of the air" (10:12). There is but one sheet that includes all creatures, both clean—what may be eaten—and unclean—what may not be eaten—as stipulated by Jewish Torah. Peter, a Torah-observant Jew, immediately recognizes the mixing of clean and unclean animals for food. So, when the voice tells him to kill and eat, he immediately responds, "By no means, Lord; for I have never eaten anything that is profane or unclean" (10:14). The voice replies, "What God has made clean, you must not call profane" (10:15).

Once Cornelius' slaves arrive, Peter continues to ponder the meaning of his vision. After hearing the slaves' request, he goes to Joppa the next day to meet Cornelius. Peter addresses Cornelius' household, relatives, and close friends, saying, "You yourselves know that it is unlawful for a Jew to associate with or to visit a Gentile; but God has shown me that I should not call anyone profane or unclean" (10:28). In other words, Peter is gradually coming to understand the meaning of his vision. Then, Cornelius narrates his vision to Peter: "Four days ago at this very hour, at three o'clock, I was praying in my house when suddenly a man in dazzling clothes stood before me" (10:30). He continues to narrate the words the angel told him, saying, "Cornelius, your payer has been heard and your alms have been remembered before God" (10:31).

After Cornelius further explains his vision and how he came to invite Peter to his house, Peter gives a speech, like he did at the beginning of the Acts of the Apostles that prepares for the Gentile Pentecost and further explains the meaning of his vision. "I truly understand that God shows no partiality, but in every nation anyone who fears him and does what is right is acceptable to him," states Peter (10:34–35). Then, after giving one of the most compact summaries of early Christian preaching ever penned, the narrator writes: "While Peter was still speaking, the Holy Spirit fell upon all who heard the word" (10:44). The Jewish-Christian believers who had accompanied Peter were, of course, astounded that the Holy Spirit had been given to the Gentiles, but they could not deny it because it was accompanied by signs similar to the Jewish Pentecost narrated in chapter two of the Acts. After this, Peter instructs that water be brought and the Gentiles baptized in the name of Jesus Christ.

The meaning of Peter's visionary prayer unfolds only with time. While being prayerful, he has a vision. He does not know what the vision means, but he is open to the events that follow it. It is his openness that allows the meaning of the vision to unfold. Accepting the invitation of Cornelius' slaves and arriving in the home of a Gentile raises Peter's awareness of the meaning of the vision. And after recounting the basic elements of Jewish Christianity, the meaning of the vision is confirmed by the falling of the Holy Spirit upon all who were gathered in Cornelius' home.

Likewise for modern believers, interpreting a vision unfolds gradually. One may be standing in a grocery store, notice the high price of an item, and suddenly become aware of the poor. Being open to other events, like an invitation to work in a soup kitchen or carry donations to a food pantry, may explain the meaning of the vision. Being caught up in prayer and song during Mass may unfold itself as a call to priesthood or religious life. Even a walk down the street may open a person to the need to volunteer in some way. If opportunities suddenly present themselves, the meaning of the vision becomes clear. Peter's visionary prayer teaches that the meaning of a vision unfolds gradually.

Meditation: Choose a vision that you have had and identify the steps in understanding its meaning. What was the vision? What was the first step in understanding its meaning? What was the second, third, etc.? How long did it take for the meaning of the vision to unfold for you?

Prayer: LORD God, you open heaven in order to give visions to your people that direct their lives according to your will. Let the Holy Spirit fall upon me in prayer, that I may receive your word in openness and patiently await the unfolding of its meaning in my life. I ask this through my Lord Jesus Christ, your Son, who lives and reigns with you and the Holy Spirit, one God, forever and ever. Amen.

RETELLING VISIONARY PRAYER
(11:2–5a, 18)

Scripture: "... [W]hen Peter went up to Jerusalem, the circumcised believers criticized him, saying, 'Why did you go to uncircumcised men and eat with them?' Then Peter began to explain it to them, step by step, saying, 'I was in the city of Joppa praying, and in a trance I saw a vision.' When they heard this, they were silenced. And they praised God, saying, 'Then God has given even to the Gentiles the repentance that leads to life.'" (Acts 11:2–5a, 18)

Reflection: Sometimes the meaning of visionary prayer becomes clearer for the visionary and those listening to the steps of its narrative through a retelling. That is what Peter does once he leaves Cornelius' home and returns to Jerusalem. The Jewish Christians in Jerusalem know nothing of Peter's vision; all they know is that he has been breaking the Torah by associating with Gentiles, uncircumcised men. In order for the circumcised to understand why Peter did this, he retells the details of his vision, Cornelius' vision, and the experience of the Holy Spirit falling upon the Gentiles.

There are elements in Peter's retelling that further interpret the meaning of Peter's vision. In the course of rehearsing the steps of chapter ten of the Acts, Peter adds another layer of meaning: "... I remembered the word of the Lord, how he had said, 'John baptized with water, but you will be baptized with the Holy Spirit'" (11:16). In other words, Peter recognizes that Jesus' words have been fulfilled through his openness to understanding his vision.

Peter also understands more deeply that the admission of the Gentiles to this Jewish–Christian movement is all God's doing or mission. He asks his hearers, "If then God gave [the Gentiles] the same gift that he gave us when we believed in the Lord Jesus Christ, who was I that I could hinder God?" (11:17) In other words, this is God's plan that continues to unfold gradually, and Peter is the vehicle for God's gift to be given to the world.

Not only has Peter come to a deeper understanding of the meaning of his vision, but his circumcised listeners have grown in wisdom, too. They are silenced; that is, in such an understanding of the work of God, they can say nothing. All they can do is praise God for having given to the Gentiles the opportunity to turn from their former way of life toward God, the source of all life. They come to a deeper understanding of exactly how merciful their God is; not only does he desire that the Jews turn to him, but he desires that the Gentiles do the same. Thus, Peter's vision means that a redefinition of what will become Christianity is taking place; it will include Jews and Gentiles.

Meditation: Retell a vision that you have experienced in prayer. If there is no one to listen to you, write it or rewrite it on a piece of paper or in your journal. When finished, ask yourself: What is new in the retelling? What further meanings have I discovered? What are the implications for my new meanings?

Part 2

Prayer: Merciful God, after granting the grace of repentance to the Jews you also offered it to the Gentiles to demonstrate your love for your people. Shower upon me the Spirit of understanding that I may recount my experiences of your presence and come to know their meaning for my life. This prayer is made to you through Jesus Christ, your Son, who lives and reigns with you and the Holy Spirit, one God, forever and ever. Amen.

PRAYING CHURCH
(12:1–5): Monday of the Fourth Week of Easter, Years I & II

Scripture: ". . . King Herod laid violent hands upon some who belonged to the church. He had James, the brother of John, killed with the sword. After he saw that it pleased the Jews, he proceeded to arrest Peter also. (This was during the festival of Unleavened Bread.) When he had seized him, he put him in prison and handed him over to four squads of soldiers to guard him, intending to bring him out to the people after the Passover. While Peter was kept in prison, the church prayed fervently to God for him." (Acts 12:1–5)

Reflection: The narrative about Peter's arrest and imprisonment and a few verses later about his release are the second to last scenes involving Peter in the Acts of the Apostles. The narrator then turns his attention to Paul, the apostle to the Gentiles. In order to remove Peter from the story, the author explains how King Herod, Agrippa I, grandson of Herod the Great, functions like his ancestors. Just as Herod Antipas (also known as Herod the Tetrarch), son of Herod the Great, had John the Baptist imprisoned and beheaded, so does Agrippa I have James, one of the twelve apostles, arrested and beheaded. This act pleases the Jewish majority of Jerusalem which inspires Herod Agrippa I to seize Peter, too.

Peter, like Jesus, is arrested at the time of Passover. The author of Acts seems to collapse Passover and the seven days of Unleavened Bread that follow it. His interest is portraying a different kind of passover that is achieved through fervent prayer. Once Peter is arrested and imprisoned, the church prays fervently to God for him, much like Jesus prayed fervently before his arrest on the Mount of Olives. While Peter is powerless in prison, the prayer of the community is powerful enough to bring about a passover, namely, Peter's miraculous escape.

The apostles had already been set free from prison by an angel of the Lord earlier in Acts. Thus, it comes as no surprise to the reader that the church's prayers are answered by another angel of the Lord, who awakens Peter and leads him past the guards and out of the prison. Peter's passover occurs on "the very night before Herod was going to bring him out" (12:6), that is, arouse the Jews to seek his death at Herod's hands, like James a few days before. Once Peter is free, he goes "to the house of Mary, the mother of John whose other name was Mark, where many had gathered and were praying" (12:12). In other words, Peter goes to the praying church to acknowledge that her prayer has been answered.

Except for Peter's appearance and short speech during the assembly in Jerusalem (15:7–11), which recounts his launching of the mission to the Gentiles, this is the last scene featuring Peter in the Acts of the Apostles.

The praying church reminds the reader that prayer is not just an individual activity; it is also a community endeavor. When the church is at fervent prayer, the action is referred to as liturgy, a Greek word meaning "the people's work." Liturgy is the Holy Spirit's expression through people functioning as the one body of Christ ritually and publically. Liturgical prayer is the epitome of the Christian life. The *Catechism of the Catholic Church* says,

> Prayer and the Christian life are inseparable, for they concern the same love and the same renunciation, proceeding from love; the same filial and loving conformity with the Father's plan of love; the same transforming union in the Holy Spirit who conforms [people] more and more to Christ Jesus . . . .[9]

---

9. Ibid., par. 2745.

Part 2

The praying church becomes visible primarily during sacramental celebrations. Baptism, Confirmation, and Eucharist—the sacraments of initiation—transform the body of Christ through liturgical prayer by adding members, filling them with the Holy Spirit, and confirming their identity as Christians. The sacraments of healing—Penance and Anointing of the Sick—find the praying church members forgiving each other and seeking the healing of its ailing members. In the sacraments of vocation—Marriage and Holy Orders—the praying church witnesses the life-long vows of man and woman and confirms the choice of her leaders.

There are other liturgical celebrations, such as Eucharistic Adoration and Benediction, the Dedication of a Church and an Altar, the religious profession of men as brothers and women as sisters, the annual Chrism Mass celebrated by the bishop of a diocese on Holy Thursday, etc. In all liturgical celebrations, signs of God's presence abound. Such signs include water, oil, bread, wine, and the laying on of hands. As demonstrated in the Acts of the Apostles, the praying church, the body of Christ, has its prayer answered.

Meditation: When have you last participated in the praying church? What liturgy was it? What were the signs of God's presence?

Prayer: Father of my Lord Jesus Christ, you always hear and answer the prayer of your Son. As a member of his body, I ask that you enliven my prayer with the Holy Spirit and join it with him, who lives and reigns with you and the Holy Spirit, one God, forever and ever. Amen.

COMMISSIONING PRAYER
(13:1–4)

Scripture: "Now in the church at Antioch there were prophets and teachers: Barnabas . . . and Saul. While they were worshiping the Lord and fasting, the Holy Spirit said, 'Set apart for me Barnabas

Prayer in the Acts of the Apostles

and Saul for the work to which I have called them.' Then after fasting and praying they laid their hands on them and sent them off. So, being sent out by the Holy Spirit, they went [forth] . . . ." (Acts 13:1–4)

Reflection: While the members of the church at Antioch are worshiping and fasting, the Holy Spirit directs them to set apart Barnabas and Saul for mission. The author does not tell us in what kind of worship the community is engaged, but he does indicate that it is liturgy or public worship. Since the Holy Spirit dwells within the community, he expresses himself best when the community is praying together.

The author weaves into this narrative one of his favorite themes, namely, fasting and praying, marks of Jewish piety. Following the bidding of the Holy Spirit, the community members lay their hands on the head of Barnabas and Saul, thus commissioning them with the authority they need to proclaim the gospel. Then, they are sent on their way both by the community and the Holy Spirit, who functions and expresses himself within and through the community or church.

Commissioning prayer, as narrated in the Acts of the Apostles, delegates others and gives them the authority to proclaim the gospel. Both Barnabas and Paul (as the narrator now refers to Saul) are called apostles by the author of Acts, yet they are not members of the twelve. The word "apostle" means "sent." Thus, Barnabas and Paul, like the twelve before them sent by Jesus, are sent by the Holy Spirit and the community of believers in Antioch with the good news of the kingdom of God.

The pattern established in this commissioning prayer—worship, fasting, prayer, imposition of hands—becomes the model for the ordination of bishops and priests. Bishops are understood to be the successors of the apostles, and priests are understood to be the bishops' helpers. Their ordination occurs during liturgy, hopefully after they have spent time in fasting and prayer. Three bishops imposed their hands upon the head of a priest and declare that the Trinitarian God has called him to the office of bishop. One bishop lays his hands on the head of a deacon and declares that the Trinitarian God has called him to assist the bishop as a priest in teaching, governing, and sanctifying.

But this is not the only type of commissioning prayer. Parish Councils, Finance Councils, and Stewardship Councils are commissioned to advise pastors about decisions concerning the parish. Readers are commissioned to proclaim the word of God. Eucharistic Ministers are commissioned to share the body and blood of Christ with their brothers and sisters. Altar servers are commissioned to assist priests. Ushers and greeters are commissioned to welcome all to worship. General Intercessors are commissioned to lead the community in universal prayers. Musicians and choir members are commissioned to lead the community in song.

While in many parishes the ministers needed for liturgical prayer are usually surfaced by seeking volunteers, their very desire to serve during public prayer indicates the work of the Holy Spirit, who instructs the community to set them apart for such ministries, just like the Holy Spirit instructed the church at Antioch to set apart Barnabas and Saul.

Meditation: For what ministry or ministries have you been set apart by the Holy Spirit? What kind of commissioning prayer was prayed for you or did you pray? How do you proclaim the gospel through your ministry?

Prayer: All Holy God, through the Holy Spirit you call men and women and set them apart for work in the church. Grant me the grace to hear your call and follow in the footsteps of your Son, Jesus Christ, in proclaiming the good news of your kingdom. You live and reign as one God—Father, Son, and Holy Spirit—forever and ever. Amen.

Prayer in the Acts of the Apostles

STRENGTHENING PRAYER

(14:22–23): Fifth Sunday of Easter, Cycle C; Tuesday of the Fifth Week of Easter, Years I & II

Scripture: "There [in Antioch, Paul and Barnabas] strengthened the souls of the disciples and encouraged them to continue in the faith, saying, 'It is through many persecutions that we must enter the kingdom of God.' And after they had appointed elders for them in each church, with prayer and fasting they entrusted them to the Lord in whom they had come to believe." (Acts 14:22–23)

Reflection: By the beginning of chapter fifteen of the Acts of the Apostles, the reader notices that three groups of leaders have emerged in the early days of the church. First, there are apostles; Matthias is chosen to replace Judas, and Barnabas and Paul are chosen by the Holy Spirit for Paul's first missionary journey. Second, there are those who are appointed to wait on tables; they later become known as deacons. And third, there are elders appointed by Paul and Barnabas; they later become known as priests.

Paul and Barnabas strengthen the souls of believers in Antioch. This means that they do what Jesus told Peter to do, namely, to strengthen the faith of the apostles in the face of persecution. After the first Christian communities were formed, they needed to be stabilized, because it was easy for them to dissolve when dealing with opposition. Remaining loyal to their faith in the gospel and to their community life required more than just a visit from Paul and Barnabas.

Commitment to God's kingdom often means suffering of some kind. The model is, of course, Jesus. The disciple is like his teacher insofar as he or she willingly accepts whatever suffering, persecution, or derision comes his or her way because of his or her way of life. Because early disciples are few in number, they need strong leaders or elders who nurture and stabilize the community and serve as a reminder and representative of Paul and Barnabas. So, after prayer and fasting, like that which occurred before Paul

Part 2

and Barnabas were sent, elders are appointed for each church. These elders are entrusted to the Lord in whom they believe.

Today's elders are pastors, deacons, and parish coordinators. While they have some governing responsibility, they are primarily responsible for strengthening prayer, that is, to strengthen the souls of parishioners and encourage them to continue in faith. Their strengthening prayer flows from their own prayer and fasting and dedication to the Lord in whom they believe.

Often, a business model is used. The church is thought of as a business. It needs to sell its products, recruit buyers, and pay its bills. The business model falls very short when compared to the apostolic model presented in the Acts of the Apostles. There is nothing to sell. When suffering comes for any reason, elders strengthen the suffering, reminding them that persecution of any kind happened to Jesus and happens to his followers before entering God's kingdom. The twin disciplines of prayer and fasting, a favorite theme of the Acts of the Apostles, strengthens elders and believers in their faith in Jesus Christ.

Meditation: Who are the elders in your parish? In what ways do they strengthen you? Whom do you strengthen? For whom have you said a strengthening prayer?

Prayer: All-powerful God, from the prayer and fasting of elders, you strengthen your people to remain steadfast in faith. Let my strengthening prayer come before you for those who strengthen me and for those whom I strengthen. May I continue in the faith and boldly proclaim your kingdom, where you live and reign with your Son, Jesus Christ, and the Holy Spirit, one God, forever and ever. Amen.

PLACE OF PRAYER

(16:13–14, 16): Monday of the Sixth Week of Easter, Years I & II

Scripture: "On the sabbath day we [, Paul, Silas, and Timothy,] went outside the gate [of Philippi] by the river, where we supposed

Prayer in the Acts of the Apostles

there was a place of prayer; and we sat down and spoke to the women who had gathered there. A certain woman named Lydia, a worshiper of God, was listening to us; she was . . . a dealer in purple cloth. The Lord opened her heart to listen eagerly to what was said by Paul. One day, as we were going to the place of prayer, we met a slave-girl who had a spirit of divination and brought her owners a great deal of money by fortune-telling." (Acts 16:13–14, 16)

Reflection: Beginning in chapter sixteen, verse eleven, of the Acts of the Apostles, the third-person narrative suddenly shifts to first-person plural—"we" and "us." Biblical scholars think that this shift may indicate that the author was an eye witness to this part of the Acts or that he has access to another person's travelogue. Thus, the "we" are Paul, Silas, and Timothy, and maybe someone else.

No matter how many there are, they hear of a place or house of prayer outside the city of Philippi and take the occasion to speak to the women who have gathered there. The author is not clear on what he means by a place or house of prayer, but that does not concern the reader. People have designated a place or house of prayer by the river, and they go there to pray. Among those gathering there is Lydia, a woman of substantial means because she trades in purple cloth, which is time-consuming and expensive to make and worn by the wealthy and the royal. The narrator states that God opened her heart to listen to Paul's words, after which she and her household were baptized, much like that of Cornelius and his household by Peter earlier in the book.

Another event occurs at the place or house of prayer. There is a slave-girl, possessed by a spirit of divination, who brings great wealth to her owner. The narrator records, "While she followed Paul and us, she would cry out, 'These men are slaves of the Most High God, who proclaim to you a way of salvation'" (16:17). In Luke's Gospel, the Gerasene demoniac proclaims Jesus to be the Son of the Most High God who brings salvation. This provokes an exorcism by Jesus. Likewise, after several days, Paul exorcises the spirit from the slave-girl in the name of Jesus Christ.

Part 2

The missionaries Paul, Silas, and Timothy recognize a place or house of prayer, and two prayer events occur there. Lydia embraces the Christian faith, and the slave-girl is exorcised of her spirit. While most people associate a church, synagogue, temple, or mosque as a place of prayer, there are other places that traditionally have been called places of prayer. Among those are springs, stone circles, gardens, labyrinths, shrines, etc. As seen from this story in the Acts, a place of prayer serves to connect the pray-ers to God. This may be engendered by the silence of the place, the landscape surrounding it, the artistic expressions discovered there, the scent of the burning candles, etc., or any combination of these. Once people recognize a place of prayer, they flock to it to enter into communion with God.

Meditation: Where have you found places of prayer? Make of list of them and identify what element of the place indicated to you that it was a place of prayer. In what ways were you drawn into prayer in each of those places?

Prayer: Most High God, you reveal yourself to your creation in places of prayer. With the assistance of the Holy Spirit, guide me to these places that I may praise your name as I enter into communion with you. I ask this through my Lord Jesus Christ, your Son, who lives and reigns with you and the Holy Spirit, one God, forever and ever. Amen.

SUNG PRAYER

(16:25-26, 29-31): Tuesday of the Sixth Week of Easter, Years I & II

Scripture: "About midnight Paul and Silas were praying and singing hymns to God, and the prisoners were listening to them. Suddenly there was an earthquake, so violent that the foundations of the prison were shaken; and immediately all the doors were opened and everyone's chains were unfastened. The jailer called for lights, and rushing in, he fell down trembling before Paul and Silas. Then he brought them outside and said, 'Sirs, what must I do

Prayer in the Acts of the Apostles

to be saved?' They answered, 'Believe on the Lord Jesus, and you will be saved, you and your household.'" (Acts 16:25-26, 29-31)

Reflection: After Paul exorcised the spirit of divination from the slave-girl, her owner had Paul and Silas arrested and put in prison, because they had removed his ability to make money with her. Instead of moaning and groaning while in prison, Paul and Silas sing prayer that brings the prisoners to silence. Silas, who was an elder in Jerusalem, had been sent with Paul by the leaders there while Barnabas, Paul's former missionary companion, had gone to Cyprus with Mark. Paul's and Silas' sung prayer is answered by an epiphanic earthquake that opens all the prison doors and causes all chains to be unfastened. This account of Paul's and Silas' miraculous escape from prison is meant to echo Peter's miraculous escape earlier in Acts.

A further parallel exists in that the jailer, who knows that he is going to be in trouble if the prisoners escape and, thus, is ready to kill himself, finds all the prisoners still in place. Falling down on his knees before Paul and Silas he seeks salvation. They proclaim the Lord Jesus to him, and he takes them to his home. After washing their wounds, the Gentile jailer and his household are washed with the water of baptism as a sign of their conversion, just like Peter had converted and baptized the whole household of Cornelius earlier.

The jailer's and his family's belief is set in motion by the sung prayer of Paul and Silas. While the author of the Acts of the Apostles does not indicate what prayer Paul and Silas sang, it was most likely some of the psalms. The *Catechism of the Catholic Church* says, "The words of the psalmist, sung for God, both express and acclaim the Lord's saving works . . . ."[10] Furthermore,

> Whether hymns or prayers of lamentation or thanksgiving, whether individual or communal, whether royal chants, songs of pilgrimage of wisdom-meditations, the Psalms are a mirror of God's marvelous deeds in the

---

10. Ibid., par. 2587.

history of his people, as well as a reflections of the human experiences of the Psalmist.[11]

St. Augustine once wrote that the person who sings prays twice. While sung prayer is usually thought of in connection with liturgical celebration, there is nothing to keep a pray-er in private from singing, like Paul and Silas, about God's saving works, using psalms or hymns. An earthquake may not occur, but sung prayer can open prison doors. The prejudice door of the jailer was opened. The closed Jewish door was opened to the Gentiles for Peter and Paul. The door of fear was opened to faith for many.

Meditation: What prison door has sung prayer opened for you? What change or conversion did the open door engender in you?

Prayer: O Lord, open my lips that my prayer may arise to you. Open my heart that my words of praise may be carried to you on the notes of song. May those who hear my sung prayer about your saving work in Jesus Christ, your Son, come to faith in him, who lives and reigns with you and the Holy Spirit, one God, forever and ever. Amen.

KNEELING PRAYER
(20:36–38a): Wednesday of the Seventh Week of Easter, Years I & II

Scripture: "When [Paul] had finished speaking, he knelt down with [the elders of the church in Ephesus] and prayed. There was much weeping among them all; they embraced Paul and kissed him, grieving especially because of what he had said, that they would not see him again." (Acts 20:36–38a)

Reflection: Before Paul sets sail for Jerusalem, he calls together the elders of the church of Ephesus and delivers what biblical scholars call a farewell address. In his speech, Paul recounts his ministry, how he has been a vehicle for the Holy Spirit, how he has suffered, and how his life can serve as a model for them. He exhorts the

---

11. Ibid., par. 2559.

Prayer in the Acts of the Apostles

elders to keep watch over themselves "and over all the flock, of which the Holy Spirit has made [them] overseers, to shepherd the church of God that he obtained with the blood of his own Son" (20:28).

Once Paul finishes his farewell words, he and the elders kneel down and pray. Body posture has long been recognized as an important component of prayer. Sometimes prayer occurs while standing; sometimes the pray-er sits. A person may extend his or her hands in a stance of openness, either standing or sitting. In some traditions, dance is a form of prayer. Other postures for prayer include bowing, genuflecting, and prostrating. As indicated by Paul, kneeling is also an acceptable posture for prayer.

The kneeling prayer of Paul is meant to echo the kneeling prayer of Jesus in Luke's Gospel after he gives his farewell address to his apostles and goes to the Mount of Olives, kneels down, and prays. Kneeling prayer signifies submission to God's will. Paul is preparing for his final journey to Jerusalem, and from there as a prisoner to Rome. Jesus is preparing to die as an innocent victim on the cross.

Today, kneeling prayer takes place during liturgical celebration indicating repentance. For example, kneeling prayer occurs during Penance Services, when penitents are invited to kneel and pray together a general confession of sins. However, kneeling also signifies adoration, as during the Eucharistic Prayer or before being invited to communion. During worship of the Blessed Sacrament, the posture is kneeling.

When engaging in private prayer, the reader should consider his or her body posture. While a variety exists, as indicated above, kneeling prayer should be chosen from time to time. One can kneel by his or her chair or bed, indicating submission to God's will, repentance for his or her sins, and adoration of the Most Holy One.

Meditation: How often do you enter into kneeling prayer? Where do you kneel? In what ways does kneeling prayer assist you to pray?

Part 2

Prayer: Most Holy Lord, through the indwelling of the Holy Spirit, you reveal your will for me. Give me the grace to understand your desires and the strength to oversee my life. I submit myself to you, kneeling in your presence, and begging you to hear my prayer in the name of your Son, my Lord Jesus Christ, who lives and reigns with you and the Holy Spirit, one God, forever and ever. Amen.

BEACH PRAYER

(21:4–6)

Scripture: "We looked up the disciples [in Tyre] and stayed there for seven days. Through the Spirit they told Paul not to go on to Jerusalem. When our days there were ended, we left and proceeded on our journey; and all of them, with wives and children, escorted us outside the city. There we knelt down on the beach and prayed and said farewell to one another. Then we went on board the ship, and they returned home." (Acts 21:4–6)

Reflection: After saying good-bye to the elders of the church of Ephesus, Paul set sail for Jerusalem. Along the way he changed from one ship to another, which made a stop at Tyre to unload its cargo. While in Tyre for seven days, fellow disciples were located who, through the Spirit, warned Paul of what was going to happen to him in Jerusalem. At this point in the narrative, the author peaks the interest of the reader so he or she continues reading more of the travelogue.

While the beach prayer seems to repeat the kneeling prayer following Paul's farewell speech earlier, it also enhances the solemn religious character of Paul's journey to Jerusalem. "Pilgrimages evoke our earthly journey toward heaven and are traditionally very special occasions for renewal in prayer," states the *Catechism of the Catholic Church*.[12] After seven days in Tyre, the disciples there gather with their wives and children on the beach to pray with Paul before they send him on the next leg of his pilgrimage.

---

12. Ibid., par. 2691.

Prayer in the Acts of the Apostles

Modern people do not often associate the beach with prayer. Beaches are places for sun bathing, for volleyball, for building sand castles, for relaxing after a swim in the ocean. However, a beach can be a very good place of prayer. One can easily get caught up in the rhythm of the surf, in the sparkle of the sun on the waves, with the feel of sand on feet and toes. Water and earth can awaken one's primordial connection to the Creator; the *Catechism* says: "The Holy Spirit is the living water . . . in the heart that prays. It is he who teaches us to accept it at its source: Christ."[13] There is no better place to (re)discover the living water of the Spirit than through beach prayer, like that of the disciples with Paul in Tyre.

Meditation: Have you been to a beach? Recall the experience. Did you enter into beach prayer? How did the beach make you aware of God? How did the beach make you aware of the Holy Spirit?

Prayer: Creator God, you formed the earth with its oceans and commanded the dry land to appear, so that the ground might be separated from the water. When I go to the beach, I remember your creative act. Make me thirsty for the living water of the Holy Spirit, who flows from the ocean of your Son. I ask this through Jesus Christ, my Lord, who lives and reigns with you and the Holy Spirit, one God, forever and ever. Amen.

PRAYER TRANCE

(22:17–19)

Scripture: Paul said to the people in Jerusalem: "After I had returned to Jerusalem and while I was praying in the temple, I fell into a trance and saw Jesus saying to me, 'Hurry and get out of Jerusalem quickly, because they will not accept your testimony about me.'" (Acts 22:17–19)

Reflection: After Paul is arrested, but before he is brought into the barracks by a Roman tribune in Jerusalem, the apostle asks for

---

13. Ibid., par. 2652.

Part 2

permission to speak to the people. During the course of his speech, Paul narrates the account of his conversion on the way to Damascus and his baptism by Ananias. Then, he narrates an experience he had in Jerusalem; this experience is recorded nowhere else in the Acts of the Apostles.

Paul tells his listeners that he went to the temple to pray, and while he was praying, he fell into a trance. This account is meant to echo that of Peter falling into a trance after going to the roof to pray before he is summoned by Cornelius. Furthermore, it serves to confirm Paul's call, as a similar account of entering into a prayer trance is narrated by Isaiah in the temple which confirms Isaiah's call. It also presents Paul as one obedient to Jesus, like Isaiah was obedient to God. In other words, like Isaiah was sent by God, so Paul is sent by Jesus.

While in a prayer trance, Paul hears Jesus direct him to leave Jerusalem, because the people there would not accept Paul's testimony. Indeed, just as this was true at first, it is also true upon Paul's return to Jerusalem. In other words, the same rejection is occurring now. Paul argues that his sincerity as a persecutor of the church of God should be the ground for their acceptance of his conversion. Nevertheless, Paul hears Jesus say, "Go, for I will send you far away to the Gentiles" (22:21). Isaiah was sent as a missionary to the Israelites; Paul is sent as a missionary to the whole world, which will culminate in his trip to Rome, the end of the earth.

A prayer trance is a state of profound attention to God. It is called contemplative prayer in the *Catechism of the Catholic Church*. Contemplative prayer begins with the pray-er placing himself or herself at God's disposal, that is, opening the self to being found by God. The pray-er "agrees to welcome the love by which he [or she] is loved and . . . wants to respond to it by loving even more," states the *Catechism*.[14] The person in a prayer trance "knows that the love he [or she] is returning is poured out by the Spirit in his [or her] heart, for everything is grace from God."[15] Thus, "[c]ontemplative

---

14. Ibid., par. 2712.
15. Ibid.

prayer is the poor and humble surrender to the loving will of the Father in ever deeper union with his beloved Son."[16]

The communion between God and the pray-er that results from a prayer trance leaves the person conformed more to the likeness of the Trinitarian God. As the *Catechism* states, "Contemplative prayer is . . . the pre-eminently intense time of prayer."[17] A prayer trance is not to be interpreted according to the contemporary meaning of the word "trance," that is, as a state of partly suspended animation or inability to function or a somnolent state as in hypnosis. Rather, it is a state of intense and profound attention to and communion with God, like that of Peter with God and Paul with Jesus. It may be accompanied by side effects, such as those narrated by mystics in the Christian tradition, but those are not its purpose or focus.

Meditation: When have you entered into a prayer trance? In which ways were you conformed more to the likeness of the Trinitarian God? Were there any side effects of your prayer trance?

Prayer: Holy, Holy, Holy are you Lord God, maker of heaven and earth. All is filled with your glory. I come into your presence seeking to do your will. Remove from my heart whatever gets in your way of entering into deep communion with me. Draw me closer to you, Father, Son, and Holy Spirit, that I may be conformed more and more to your likeness. You are one God, living and reigning forever and ever. Amen.

PRAYER FOR MORE BELIEVERS

(26:27–29, 31–32)

Scripture: Paul said: "'King Agrippa, do you believe the prophets? I know that you believe.' Agrippa said to Paul, 'Are you so quickly persuading me to become a Christian?' Paul replied, 'Whether quickly or not, I pray to God that not only you but also all who are

---

16. Ibid.
17. Ibid., par. 2714.

Part 2

listening to me today might become such as I am—except for these chains.' . . . As [King Agrippa, Bernice, and Porcius Festus] were leaving, they said to one another, 'This man is doing nothing to deserve death or imprisonment.' Agrippa said to Festus, 'This man could have been set free if he had not appealed to the emperor.'" (Acts 26:27–29, 31–32)

Reflection: Paul is handed over the Roman government officials by the Jews, just like Jesus was. His case is heard first by Felix, who was governor of Palestine from 52 to 60 CE, in Caesarea, where Paul remains imprisoned. Felix is succeeded by Porcius Festus around 60 CE, and he hears Paul's case again in Caesarea. King Agrippa II, son of Agrippa I, and his sister, Bernice, go to Caesarea to pay their respects to the new governor, as a client king should do. Festus recounts Paul's case to Agrippa and tells him that he can find no case against him. Agrippa asks Festus if he can hear Paul, and Festus agrees.

In the course of his defense speech, Paul recounts the highlights of his life, his persecution of the followers of Jesus of Nazareth, his conversion on the road to Damascus, and his mission to the Gentiles. Festus accuses Paul of being out of his mind, but Paul turns to King Agrippa II and asks him if he believes the prophets. Agrippa knows the implication of his answer to Paul's question. If he says no, he will indicate that he doesn't know what has been going on in the territory he rules; if he says yes, then Paul is going to ask him why he doesn't believe the prophets.

Agrippa deflects Paul's question with his own question. He asks Paul, "Are you so quickly persuading me to become a Christian?" Paul, being the rhetorician he is, deflects Agrippa's counter question, by declaring that it matters not whether he believes quickly or slowly, only that he and all those listening to Paul might believe the way he does. Furthermore, Paul prays to God that this might be the case.

The similarities between Jesus' trials and Paul's trials are intended by the author of the Acts of the Apostles. In all three of his trials, Jesus is declared innocent; in all three of his trials, Paul is declared innocent. The lesson set before the pray-er is one taught by Jesus, namely, to pray for the conversion of one's abusers.

The prayer for more believers is best illustrated in liturgical prayer on Good Friday. In the Solemn Intercessions, prayers are said by the whole church for those who do not believe in Christ that the light of the Holy Spirit may show them the way to salvation. Prayers are also said for those who do not believe in God that they may find him by following all that is right. Furthermore, in the prayer for those who do not believe in God, the pray-ers petition the eternal God to let the tokens of his love and mercy shine through the lives of Christians so that non-believers may acknowledge him as the one true God and Father of all. Basically, these are summarized in Paul's prayer before King Agrippa II, that all who listen to Paul and all who witness his life lived in service of the gospel become like Paul—except without the chains.

Meditation: How often do you pray for more believers in Christ? Do you pray for those who do not believe in Christ? Do you pray for those who do not believe in God? Do God's love and mercy shine through your Christian life? How?

Prayer: God of all, you have revealed your Son to the Jews through the preaching of Peter, and you have made him known to the Gentiles through the preaching of Paul. I pray now for all who do not believe in Jesus; send the light of the Holy Spirit to lead them to salvation. I pray for all who do not believe in you, Father; let your love and mercy shine through my life, that they may come to recognize you as you are: Father, Son, and Holy Spirit, one God, forever and ever. Amen.

PRAYER FOR DAY
(27:29)

Scripture: "Fearing that we might run on the rocks, [the sailors] let down four anchors from the stern [of the ship] and prayed for day to come." (Acts 27:29)

Part 2

Reflection: Because Paul was a Roman citizen and appealed his case to the emperor, Festus, the governor of Palestine, sent him on a ship to Rome. The ship was caught in a severe storm at sea that lasted for several days. In order to keep the ship from sinking, the sailors tossed overboard all the cargo and the tackle. Now, the ship is drifting. Fourteen nights later, a vague illusion to Passover, while drifting in the sea, the sailors suspect they are nearing land. They take soundings to confirm their suspicions. Then, they drop anchors to keep the ship from running aground.

They pray for day to come so they can see where they are. The next morning they raise the anchors and run the ship aground on Malta, after Paul "took bread; and giving thanks to God in the presence of all, he broke it and began to eat" (27:35). In other words, Paul celebrated the Lord's Supper, the new passover, to commemorate the passing over that they had just done. During the night, they had escaped death, and in the light of day they arrived at Malta alive.

This account of Paul's passover is meant to echo that of Peter's earlier in the Acts. At the time of Passover, Peter is jailed, and, while the church prays for him, he is set free by an angel of the Lord. King Herod Agrippa I intended to put Peter to death, but he passed over from death to life. Paul faced death if the ship ran aground during the night, but he passed over from death to life the next day.

While not all crises occur at night, many do. More people die during the night than during the day. Traffic death rates are three times higher at night than during the day. Stroke patients who enter a hospital at night are more likely to die than those who enter during the day. More break-ins and robberies occur under cover of darkness than during the light of day. The statistics for groups, like those who drink alcohol and drive, show that more deaths take place during the night than during the day. And on and on the statistics go.

The light of day brings sight. Indeed, many people make a better decision the day after sleeping on a problem. So, praying for day does not imply merely praying for rays of sunshine. Praying for day is a metaphor for seeing clearly. If the issue concerns a child, praying for day is asking for the Holy Spirit's help to solve a problem. If the issue concerns a relationship, praying for day is seeking the Holy Spirit's insight to enhance the friendship. Praying for day may mean remembering those undergoing chemotherapy or radiation therapy for cancer, asking God to shine his rays of healing upon them. The sailors prayed for day as they passed through the night. Whatever the darkness, a prayer for day shows the way.

Meditation: When have you prayed for day during a dark night? How did you pass over through death to life? What three prayers for day do you need to say right now?

Prayer: God of light, during the night you passed over your chosen people in Egypt, so that they could emerge into your light the next day. Shine the light of the Holy Spirit in my dark nights to keep my faith strong. When dawn arrives, give me the strength to praise your name, Father, Son, and Holy Spirit, one God, forever and ever. Amen.

HEALING PRAYER
(28:7–9)

Scripture: "Now in the neighborhood of [Malta] were lands belonging to the leading man of the island, named Publius, who received us and entertained us hospitably for three days. It so happened that the father of Publius lay sick in bed with fever and dysentery. Paul visited him and cured him by praying and putting his hands on him. After this happened, the rest of the people on the island who had diseases also came and were cured." (Acts 28:7–9)

Reflection: While Paul is shipwrecked on Malta, he is shown hospitality by a certain Publius, whose father is sick in bed with a fever. It is important to note that Publius shows hospitality for three days, indicating a theophany. Indeed, the theophany occurs when Paul visits Publius' father, prays for him, and imposes his hands on him, for his father is healed. After this, word spreads and Paul heals the rest of the people on the island with diseases.

Paul's healing prayer echoes that of Jesus' healing in Luke's Gospel. Jesus heals Peter's mother-in-law. Then, many who are ill are brought to Jesus; he lays his hands on them and cures them. What occurred once in Galilee in Simon's house is now occurring in Malta in Publius' home. Paul is only three months away from arriving in Rome, where the gospel and the healing ministry of Jesus will have reached the end of the earth.

Both Penance and the Anointing of the Sick, sacraments of healing, contain the laying on of hands. While he is saying the prayer of absolution, the priest either lays his hand or hands on the head of the penitent or extends his hand or hands toward the penitent. After praying for the sick, the priest goes to each candidate for anointing and lays his hands on his or her head before anointing the person with the Oil of the Sick. The sign indicates healing.

Healing prayer can be said by anyone. One may ask God to heal his arthritis; this prayer may be answered by a doctor's prescription after seeing the patient. One may ask God to heal her mental suffering; this prayer may be answered by a counselor or spiritual director. Parents often enter into healing prayer with their children to cleanse a scraped knee or elbow. A hug between friends may be a healing prayer after a disagreement.

Jesus' ministry of healing that proclaims the presence of God's kingdom continued through the hands of Paul. Now, it continues through the hands of anyone who says a healing prayer.

Meditation: From what did you most recently ask God for healing? For whom did you recently say a healing prayer? In what ways have your healing prayers been answered?

Prayer: Mighty God, through his deeds of healing, your Son, Jesus Christ, proclaimed the presence of your kingdom. He passed on this ministry to his church. Grant healing to all in the assembly of believers, that they may recognize the coming of your kingdom, where you live and reign with my Lord Jesus Christ and the Holy Spirit, one God, forever and ever. Amen.

Other Books by Mark G. Boyer

History of St. Joachim Parish: 1822—1972; 1723—1973

Day by Day through the Easter Season

Following the Star: Daily Reflections for Advent and Christmas

Mystagogy: Liturgical Paschal Spirituality for Lent and Easter

Return to the Lord: A Lenten Journey of Daily Reflections

The Liturgical Environment: What the Documents Say

Breathing Deeply of God's New Life: Preparing Spiritually for the Sacraments of Initiation

Mary's Day—Saturday: Meditations for Marian Celebrations

Why Suffer?: The Answer of Jesus

A Month-by-Month Guide to Entertaining Angels

Biblical Reflections on Male Spirituality

"Seeking Grace with Every Step": The Spirituality of John Denver

Home Is a Holy Place

Day by Ordinary Day with Mark

Day by Ordinary Day with Matthew

Day by Ordinary Day with Luke

Baptized into Christ's Death and Resurrection: Preparing to Celebrate a Christian Funeral: Vol. 1: Adults

Baptized into Christ's Death and Resurrection: Preparing to Celebrate a Christian Funeral: Vol. 2: Children

Other Books by Mark G. Boyer

The Greatest Gift of All: Reflections and Prayers for the Christmas Season

Meditations for Ministers

Waiting in Joyful Hope: Reflections for Advent 2001

Filled with New Light: Reflections for Christmas 2001–2002

Lent and Easter Prayer at Home

Using Film to Teach New Testament

Waiting in Joyful Hope: Daily Reflections for Advent and Christmas 2002–2003

Waiting in Joyful Hope: Daily Reflections for Advent and Christmas 2003–2004

The Liturgical Environment: What the Documents Say (second edition)

Reflections on the Rosary

When Day Is Done: Nighttime Prayers through the Church Year

Take Up Your Cross and Follow: Daily Lenten Reflections

These Thy Gifts: A Collection of Simple Meal Prayers

Day by Ordinary Day: Daily Reflections on the First Readings, Year One

Day by Ordinary Day: Daily Reflections on the First Readings, Year Two

Mountain Reflections: A Collection of Photos and Meditations

Nature Spirituality: Praying with Wind, Water, Earth, Fire

A Spirituality of Ageing

Caroling through Advent and Christmas

Weekday Saints: Reflections on Their Scriptures

Human Wholeness: A Spirituality of Relationship

The Liturgical Environment: What the Documents Say (third edition)

A Simple Systematic Mariology

Index of Biblical Quotations

PSALMS

2:7	6
31:5	33
141:2	2

ISAIAH

42:1	6

LUKE

1:6	3
1:10	1
1:11–13	3
1:35	6
2:11	14
2:26	14
2:36–38	4
3:21–22	5–6
5:15–16	7
6:12–13	8
6:20, 27–28	10
6:33–35	12
9:18	13
9:20	14
9:28–29	15
9:32	31
9:35	15
10:21–22	17
11:1–2	19
11:4	31
17:21	17
18:1, 6–8	21
18:10–11, 13–14	22
19:45–46	25
21:31	27
21:34	28
21:36	27
22:3	29
22:31–32	29
22:40–45	30
23:32–24	32
23:46	33
24:52	25

ACTS

1:13–14	35
1:23–26	37
2:36	39
2:41–42	39
3:1–2	41
3:6	41
4:10	43
4:18	43
4:24–25a, 26–31	43

ACTS (continued)

6:2–4	45
6:5	47
6:6	45–46
6:8–10, 12; 7:51, 54, 58–60	47
8:9	51
8:12	49
8:14–16	49
8:18–20, 22	50–51
8:24	51–52
9:10–12	52
9:17	53
9:36–37a, 40	54
10:1–4	55–56
10:9–11, 16–17a, 19–20	57–58
10:12	58
10:14	58
10:15	58
10:28	58
10:30	58–59
10:31	59
10:34–35	59
10:44	59
11:2–5a, 18	60
11:16	61
11:17	61
12:1–5	62
12:6	63
12:12	63
13:1–4	64–65
14:22–23	67
16:13–14, 16	68–69
16:17	69
16:25–26, 29–31	70–71
20:28	73
20:36–38a	72
21:4–6	74
22:17–19	75
22:21	76
26:27–29, 31–32	77–78
27:29	79
27:35	80
28:7–9	81

www.ingramcontent.com/pod-product-compliance
Lightning Source LLC
Chambersburg PA
CBHW070514090426
42735CB00012B/2773